M000281232

STRANGE BUT TRUE
SOUTH CAROLINA

SWEETWATER
PRESS

Strange But True South Carolina

Copyright © 2007 Cliff Road Books, Inc.

Produced by arrangement with Sweetwater Press

Ripley's Aquarium® is a registered trademark of Ripley's Entertainment Inc.

ISBN-13: 978-1-58173-522-2
ISBN-10: 1-58173-522-7

Design by Miles G. Parsons
Map of South Carolina by Tim Rocks

Printed in The United States of America

LYNNE L. HALL

SWEETWATER
PRESS

TABLE OF CONTENTS

In a Strange State:

Road Trip Through Strange But True South Carolina

Smiling faces. Beautiful places. That's how the folks at the South Carolina tourism department want you to see their state. Read their colorful brochures, watch their sophisticated travel commercials, and you'll be regaled by the state's many beautiful sights. And, no doubt about it, there's plenty to see.

The quintessential Southern state, South Carolina is filled with Southern charm and friendliness, so much so, in fact, that Columbia, the state capital, is known as the Capital of Southern Hospitality. Smiling faces everywhere.

And everywhere are beautiful places. Along South Carolina's eastern edge you'll find sandy white beaches awash with the diamond-sparkle of the Atlantic Ocean. This lowcountry area is filled to the gills with fecund wildlife estuaries and dotted by the Carolina bays, picturesque inlets experts believe were formed by an ancient meteor shower.

Traveling inland, you'll find charming Southern towns, where you'll stroll down wisteria-lined streets, past stately antebellum homes. Then, wend your way up through the Sand Hill region and north through the rolling Foothills of the Piedmont area. Up and up you climb, past wooded landscapes, sparkling lakes, and cascading waterfalls; up shady winding roadways to the summit of Sassafras Mountain, the top of the state. Here, you'll have to remind yourself to catch your breath as you take in the awe-inspiring vistas of the historic Blue Ridge Mountains.

That's the tourism department's South Carolina—beautiful, elegant, stately.

Ah, but there's another South Carolina lurking behind all that loveliness and sophistication and it's a state of pure wackiness, a place filled with madcap characters, zany attractions, and screwball adventures. Forget purple mountain majesties and shady country lanes. We got the world's only UFO Information Center, a crab on steroids, lobsters that race, and a whole slew of weirded-out museums (Our favorite is the dental museum. It's a really numbing experience!) Oh! And you won't want to miss that Chitlin' Strut, possibly the world's weirdest festival.

So drop that colorful brochure. Turn off the slick television commercial and join us on a journey down the back roads of Strange But True South Carolina.

Strange Statues

We've Got Statues

Scattered willy-nilly across Strange But True South Carolina is an eclectic collection of strange and quirky monuments.

BASEBALL WATER TOWER • FORT MILL

The Giants have lost their ball. Oh, wait. They play football, don't they? Anyway, there's a giant baseball in Fort Mill. The baseball tower represents the minor league team the Charlotte Knights. Yes, you're right to be confused. Charlotte is, indeed, in North Carolina. However, Fort Mill is only a few miles from Charlotte, and this is where Knights Stadium is located. Hence the giant baseball tower.

Built to accommodate an expansion team in the International League, the stadium is a state-of-the-art facility that seats ten thousand.

Located at 2280 Deerfield Drive.

CLAYTON "PEG LEG" BATES • FOUNTAIN INN

The next time you hear yourself whine "I can't," take a moment to reflect on the life of Clayton Bates. Clayton was born to Fountain Inn sharecroppers in the early 1900s. Times were pretty tough, but they got even tougher when his father abandoned the family, leaving the responsibility for feeding his children to Clayton's mother.

Despite existing in abject poverty, Clayton was a light-hearted child who somehow discovered a love and a talent for dance. By the age of five, he was earning nickels entertaining audiences in the streets of Fountain Inn and dreaming of someday becoming a professional dancer.

Unfortunately, even back then, nickels didn't go very far, so at age twelve Clayton went to work in a local farm factory to help put food on the family table. He had worked only a few days when times got even tougher.

Bates was working in a cotton gin one day, when he slipped and caught his left leg in a conveyor belt. The leg was badly mangled, but in those days there was no hospital for African-Americans. The young hoofer was taken home and, on the kitchen table where he ate his supper every night, his leg was amputated below the knee.

His uncle whittled him a wooden leg, and immediately Clayton began practicing, teaching himself a unique brand of peg leg tap dancing. Within a year, he was once again entertaining audiences in the streets. It wasn't long before his wooden leg matched the ability of his other leg.

Determined to pursue his dream, Clayton, by then cleverly nicknamed "Peg Leg" by the townsfolk, moved with his mother to Greenville, where he danced at county fairs and carnivals. He spent seven years there, dancing, entertaining, and perfecting his steps. He was quite the accomplished dancer when, one night in 1927, a New York producer saw him dance at the Greenville Black Liberty Theater. Maybe it was the signature step that wowed him. Called the "Imitation American Jet

Plane," the step was a five-foot leap into the air, with Peg Leg landing on his peg leg, his good leg extended straight out. Pretty impressive. At least the producer thought so. He "discovered" Clayton "Peg Leg" Bates there in Greenville and took him straight away to New York. And the rest is history.

Peg Leg's dream of becoming a professional dancer was realized. He did, in fact, become a world-famous tap dancer. He traveled the globe, tapping and leaping and entertaining. In 1951, Peg Leg decided it was time to retire. Throughout his world travels, there were many times when he had not been allowed to stay in the resorts in which he was performing because of the color of his skin. Perhaps that was his motivation in now establishing a resort in the Catskills. The resort, named Peg Leg Bates Country Club, became a popular hot spot, with famous entertainers performing there. Peg Leg operated the resort until the eighties, when he turned it over to his daughter.

In December of 1998 at age ninety-one, Peg Leg visited Fountain Inn and danced at a fund raiser held to raise money for his statue. He died of a heart attack the next day. The money was eventually raised, and Fountain Inn did, indeed, erect a fine statue of him. You can see it in all its glory in the downtown area.

AMELIA BEDELIA • MANNING

Amelia Bedelia is the brain child of writer Peggy Parish, a Manning native. In this series of children's books, Amelia Bedelia is a maid who works for the wealthy Rogerses. Unfortunately for them, Amelia takes things literally and is always screwing up her assignments. Luckily, she is an excellent cook, and the family loves to eat, so in the end Amelia gets to keep her job.

Parish, who was a teacher, uses the series to help teach children that words can have multiple meanings, one of which may be preferred over the other. The books are useful in teaching children about semantics, particularly idioms and metaphors. Although Parish died unexpectedly in 1988, Amelia lives on, now written by Parish's nephew, Herman. She continues to be popular with kids around the world.

To honor Parish, a statue of Amelia, wearing a floppy flowered hat, with a purse on her shoulder, and a kitty by her side, has been placed outside the Clarendon County Library in Manning. The life-size bronze sculpture was sculpted by Clarendon County artist Jim Chaconas, who volunteered his time and skill to the project.

Located at 215 North Brook Street.

CIVITAS STATUES • ROCK HILL

Rock Hill, South Carolina, might be the last place you'd expect to find four Greek goddesses, but, hey, there they stand in all their glory. The four thirteen-foot-tall bronze statues are the pride and joy of this once-tiny community, now one of the state's fastest-growing cities. Sculpted by artist Audrey Flack, the goddesses anchor the circular Gateway Plaza and embody the city's dedication to its heritage and to growth and progress.

Flack chose the image of strong women to represent Rock Hill's dedication to its civic planning program titled,

"Empowering the Vision," begun in 1988. Each statue holds aloft a disc containing symbols of the city's strength. One holds the stars of inspiration, symbolizing the city's dedication to culture. One holds the flame of knowledge, symbolizing education, represented by Winthrop University, one of Rock Hill's largest employers. Another goddess holds the gears of industry. And the last one holds lightning bolts to symbolize the utilities represented by another

Rock Hill has four goddess statues in Gateway Plaza.
Copyright Audrey Flack, 1990.
Courtesy of the city of Rock Hill.

large employer, the Catawba Nuclear Plant. Their wings and hair resemble folds of fabric, reflecting Rock Hill's heritage in the textile industry.

Anyway, the statues were erected at Gateway Plaza in 1991 and a fifth statue was placed in the rotunda encompassing City Hall a year later. They've become quite the tourist attraction since, along with the surrounding sixty-foot Egyptian Revival columns. Architect Michael Gallis scavenged the columns when Charlotte's historic Masonic Temple was razed several years ago. Nothing like a little recycling, eh?

Strange Statues

You can find it all in the Gateway Plaza on Dave Lyle Boulevard.

COW • BEAUFORT

It's a blue moo moo! Standing outside the Arts Council of Beaufort County, the cow is one of many that vacationed here from Chicago a few years ago. See, the city of Chicago sponsored a Cows on Parade art exhibit, where hundreds of life-size fiberglass cows were decorated by local artists. The cows were paraded around Chicago for several months, then were "sent on vacation" to other states, where they were auctioned off for various causes.

The Arts Council's moo moo is blue. I mean sky blue. Everything from the tip of her long horns (yes, cows do have horns) to the tip of her tail is a really bright shade of blue. We're just wondering where Paul Bunyan is.

Located at 905 Port Republic Street.

The blue cow was once part of the Cows on Parade art exhibit in Chicago.
Courtesy of the Art Council of Beaufort.
Kevin Palmer, sculptor.

EDDIE • COLUMBIA

Wondering what goes on inside that big kid of yours? Well, hie yourself on over to the Edventure Children's Museum, where you can take a trip through EDDIE.

Talk about a big kid! EDDIE is forty feet tall and weighs seventeen and a half tons! He's twice the size of both the Lincoln Memorial and the Jefferson Memorial in Washington, D.C. And he's the star of the Edventure Children's Museum.

Crafted to be a typical ten-year-old, EDDIE allows children to use gross motor skills to discover what

EDDIE helps children learn about the human body's inner workings.
Courtesy of Edventure Children's Museum.

goes on inside the human body. He sits in the middle of the museum where you can climb inside and scale EDDIE's vertebrae to his brain. Crawl through his heart. Then bounce inside his big ol' tummy. Oh, yeah, and guess where you exit? Right! You slide right out of his intestines. EWWW!

Located at 211 Gervais Street.

Strange Statues

JOHN BERKS "DIZZY" GILLESPIE • CHERAW

If jazz is your bag, one look at the enormous puffed-out cheeks and the bent horn and you'll recognize the bronze statue in the town square as bebop great Dizzy Gillespie, who was born in Cheraw in 1917.

An African-American Baha'i jazz trumpeter, composer, and singer, Gillespie taught himself to play the trumpet at age twelve. Despite growing up in extreme poverty, Gillespie won a scholarship to Laurinburg Institute in North Carolina. However, he dropped out of school and left for Philadelphia, desperate to play music for a living.

One of his first gigs was as a member of Cab Calloway's band. A gifted improviser, he often drew criticism from Calloway for his innovative solos, which Calloway called "Chinese music." It was Gillespie's hot temper, however, rather than his cool licks that lost him his job with Calloway. Seems ol' Cab accused him of hitting him in the head with a spitball during a show. Gillespie stabbed him in the leg.

Gillespie moved on to bands more appreciative of his solo talents. He began jamming in such clubs as New York's Minton Playhouse, where, along with Charlie Parker, he experimented with a hep new sound they called bebop. The sound was so radically different from the popular jazz of the day that it was first considered threatening. Gillespie's comically puffed cheeks—a technical no-no—his horn bent at a forty-five degree angle (the product of an accident that pleasantly changed the sound), scat singing, and pleasant personality were instrumental in popularizing the new sound.

Despite being known as the Father of Bebop, playing in the White House for eight different Presidents, and the many awards he won, including a star on Hollywood's Walk of Stars, Gillespie never forgot his hometown. Before every concert, he humbly introduced himself as Dizzy Gillespie from Cheraw, South Carolina.

On the eighty-fifth anniversary of Gillespie's birth, Cheraw erected a memorial statue on the town green in front of the Visitor's Center. In

Cheraw erected a statue in honor of the famed "Dizzy" Gillespie.
Courtesy of Cheraw Visitors Bureau.

addition, eight steel bench sculptures created by local students pay homage to Gillespie in the front of his birthplace at 334 Hugar Street, now known as Dizzy Gillespie Birthplace Park.

ANDREW JACKSON • LANCASTER COUNTY

North Carolina tries to claim Andrew Jackson as a native son, but South Carolinians know better. It's true our seventh president was born in the Waxhaw area, which borders both states, but Jackson called himself a native South Carolinian in his last will and testament. And that's good enough for us!

Strange Statues

South Carolina honors its native son with a state park named for him, the focus of which is an equestrian statue created by famed sculptress Anna Hyatt Huntington. Back in 1967, local school children mounted a letter-writing campaign imploring Huntington to sculpt the work. She was ninety years old when she completed the ten-foot sculpture. She titled the sculpture *Boy of Waxhaws*. It's on display in the museum at the Andrew Jackson State Park.

Located at 196 Andrew Jackson State Park Road.

South Carolina is known as the Palmetto State for the state tree, the Sabal Palmetto. This tree played a historical role during the Revolutionary War. On July 28, 1776, the British fleet attacked Sullivan Island. They didn't get far with their attack, however, for their cannonballs just bounced off the spongy, wet Palmetto logs of the fort. The Palmetto is the official state tree and appears on the state flag and the state seal.

"SHOELESS" JOE JACKSON • GREENVILLE

Joe Jackson was one of the best baseball players that ever lived. He began playing in 1908, moving up and down between the minors and the majors and gaining his "Shoeless" nickname during a game when new shoes rubbed painful blisters on his feet. He played in his socks, and while on third base, a fan called him a shoeless son-of-a-gun.

In 1911, Jackson batted .408, the highest average ever by a rookie. His lifetime batting average was .356, baseball history's third highest. Ted Williams called him the greatest natural hitter of all time and Babe Ruth admitted to copying his batting stance. Best of all, he was born in Pickens County and called Greenville home later—after the scandal.

Oh, yeah. The scandal. It all happened during the 1919 World Series, when eight members of the Chicago White Sox, including Joe Jackson, were banned from playing baseball for life for conspiring to throw the series. It was called the Black Sox Scandal and as a result, none of the eight could ever be inducted into the Baseball Hall of Fame.

There's some confusion over Jackson's participation, despite the fact that he admitted to receiving $5,000 for the fix. He also insisted he tried twice to return the money because it was dirty money, but was told to keep it. He insisted he played his best in the series. Greenville residents point out that he batted .375, hitting the only home run, throwing out five runners, and handling thirty chances in the outfield with no errors.

Others, however, point to the fact that he also batted far worse in the five games the White Sox lost to the Cincinnati Reds, totaling only one RBI. In addition, the Reds hit an unusually high number of triples to left field, way over the number Jackson usually allowed.

Jackson felt disgraced. He returned to South Carolina and reportedly played in local minor leagues under another name. He finally settled in Greenville, where he opened a liquor store and became a much beloved figure in town. He protested his innocence until the day he died. Reportedly his last words were, "This is it, good buddy. I'm going to meet the greatest umpire of all now. I know he will judge me innocent."

There's no doubt the town of Greenville has found Jackson innocent. Just look at all the ways they've found to honor him. Let's see…There's the Shoeless Joe Jackson Plaza, with a life-size statue of the great player; the Shoeless Joe Jackson Memorial Park, where he's buried; and a Shoeless Joe Jackson Memorial Parkway. There's also a push by Greenville residents and Jackson's relatives to have the ban on induction into the Baseball Hall of Fame lifted.

The statue of Jackson was sculpted by local artist Doug Young. Residents were able to participate in its creation by kneading the clay Young used in the sculpture. The statue was bronzed and then set atop a platform built from bricks from old Comisky Park.

The statue is located in Shoeless Joe Jackson Plaza at the south end of Augusta and Main streets.

JAMES ROBERT "RADIO" KENNEDY • ANDERSON

The 2003 movie *Radio* may have been named for Anderson native James Robert Kennedy, and, true, it is the story of his life. But it's even more the story of T. L. Hanna High School Coach Harold Jones, a man who, in a time before consciousness-raising, existed on a higher plane than his fellow citizens.

In 1964, James Kennedy was seventeen years old. Nicknamed "Radio" because of his fascination for transistor radios, he was an oddity and an object of ridicule in the small town of Anderson. Back then, he would have been called mentally retarded rather than developmentally challenged. He pushed around a shopping cart all day and since he never spoke, was assumed to be mute. He was unmercifully teased by children and adults alike.

But life changed for Radio when Coach Jones caught sight of him watching football practice one sunny afternoon. Instead of joining in the pettiness of fellow citizens, Jones made a conscious decision to befriend the young man. After all the teasing Radio had endured, it took some time for Jones to gain his trust, but the coach persevered and soon Radio was helping out with football practice and was even sitting in on some of the coach's academic classes.

Initially, school officials and members of the community objected to Jones's inclusion of Radio in school activities. They tried to have him barred from the school and at one point tried to have him remanded to a mental health facility. Jones fought these small-minded people and eventually won Radio a place at the school and in the hearts of Anderson's citizens. Because of the relationship, Radio was able to transcend expectations of him. He learned to talk and learned to take care of himself. In learning the value of friendship and family from Radio, Jones's life, too, was enriched.

The world learned of the story between Radio and Jones when an article published in *Sports Illustrated* caught the eye of a movie producer. The movie was released in 2003 and brought instant fame to Radio, Jones, and the town of Anderson.

Strange Statues

Inspired by the movie, sculptor Andy Davis came up with the idea for a life-sized bronze sculpture to honor Radio. Ed Harris, the actor who played Coach Jones in the movie, contributed to the completion of the project. Radio, a big grin plastered on his face, unveiled the statue on April 19, 2006. Temporarily housed in the Medicus Sculpture Garden of the Anderson County Arts Warehouse, it will eventually be moved to the high school campus.

Radio, who turned sixty in 2006, continues his relationship with the high school. Coach Jones, who had been promoted to athletic director, left in 1998, when the school's principal decided someone with experience in all sports was needed. He continues to live in Anderson and is still a good friend of Radio's.

MEDIEVAL CASTLE TOWER • BELTON

Looking for a knight in shining armor? Maybe you'll find him in Belton. There's a water tower that looks like his castle. Built in 1909, it's 155 feet tall and has a capacity of 165,000 gallons of water.

A water tower in Belton resembles a medieval castle turret. Courtesy of the South Carolina Department of Parks, Recreation, and Tourism, DiscoverSouthCarolina.com.

Located at the intersection of McGee Way and Campbell Street.

MERMAIDS • BEAUFORT

There are mermaids in Beaufort! They're swimming all over the city! The one hundred life-sized fiberglass sculptures were created by artist Kevin Palmer and were painted and decorated by local artists and citizens. They were then placed throughout downtown Beaufort, providing a scenic walking tour of the city.

Mermaids line the streets of Beaufort.
Courtesy of Beaufort, SC.

The project was sponsored by the Arts Council of Beaufort, which provided mermaid decorating classes and encouraged artists to submit their designs for consideration. Rampant imagination was encouraged, so there's no telling just what you'll find these mermaids wearing.

The mermaids began appearing along Beaufort streets in August 2006. Their official unveiling took place on October 2006 and they will remain in Beaufort, welcoming visitors and residents alike, until October 2007, when they'll be auctioned off. Sounds like a fishy project to us!

Strange Statues

MICE ON MAIN • GREENVILLE

Greenville's just full of the sneaky little rodents. But don't worry. These aren't the furry, disease-carrying ones. These little critters are made of bronze and they're fun and educational.

It all started with an idea from a creative Greenville high school student who came up with a way to make the downtown area interesting for kids and adults alike. The idea was inspired by the popular children's book, *Goodnight, Moon*, in which a sweet little bunny, in the process of going to sleep, says goodnight to everything in his room, including a recurring mouse.

Greenville's whimsical Mice on Main offer a way to explore Main Street while in the process of hunting for the hidden mice. The project starts at the fountain in front of the Hyatt Regency Hotel, where there's a bronzed sculpture of the book and one bronze mouse. The other eight mice are hidden within a nine-block stretch of Main Street between the Hyatt and the Westin Poinsett hotel. The object is to search up and down Main Street—both sides—to locate the mice. Just to keep things going, Greenville's mice tenders periodically move the mice to a different location. It's a great way to keep the kiddies as well as adults occupied.

The thrill of discovery will have you changing ol' Jinks the Cat's ('member him? If so, we're bettin' you have an AARP card!) favorite exclamation. Instead of hating them, you'll be saying, "I love meeses to pieces!"

Start at the Hyatt Regency at 220 North Main.

MIGHTY CASEY • ROCK HILL

Say, hey! It's another disgraced baseball player. We're not sure why Rock Hill chose the Mighty Casey, the fallen hero of Ernest Lawrence Thayer's 1887 epic poem, to honor but there he stands, a glorious monument to the Boys of Summer.

Remembering your baseball lore, you'll recall things didn't look brilliant for Mudville that day. It was the bottom of the ninth. They were down four to two and there were two outs. If only their mightiest hitter, the Mighty Casey, could make it to bat, there was a whisper of a chance. But, alas, two of Mudville's worst hitters were to bat before Casey. It didn't look good.

But a miracle occurred! The first batter singled and the next batter blasted a double. Now a man stood on third and another hugged second. And the Mighty Casey was up to bat.

With the crowd going wild, the big man tapped the plate and hit his stance. The pitch flew through the air. "Steeeriike!" yelled the ump and the crowd wanted

Rock Hill honors Mighty Casey from Ernest-Lawrence Thayer's poem. Courtesy of the city of Rock Hill.

to kill him. And, again, the pitch flew past him. "Steeerike Two!" The crowd held its breath—sure the next one was outta there! The pitcher did his windup and with force sent the ball sailing. As it flew past the plate, the batter took his swing. And a mighty swing it was, but, alas, it was a mighty swing and a miss. And, as the story goes, despite all his clout, no joy came to Mudville that night, for the Mighty Casey had struck out.

Rock Hill's statue of the Mighty Casey leaning casually on the instrument of his disgrace stands at the entrance of the town's Cherry Park.

Located at 1466 Cherry Road.

Peachoid Water Tower • Gaffney

Why is there a giant orange butt in the sky over Gaffney? Oh, wait. It's a peach! Actually it's a water tank that looks like a peach. South Carolina is the nation's largest producer of peaches and Gaffney is the center of much of that production. Their water tank was built to honor that humble crop.

It is, no doubt, a fitting tribute. There's just one little caveat. See, from certain angles, the big cleft down the center gives the big peach the appearance of a large derriere floating around in the Gaffney sky.

Joel Poinsett • Greenville

Joel Poinsett was a great man. A physician-turned-statesman, he served first in the South Carolina State Legislature, then went on to represent the state in the U.S. Congress. He was the U.S. Secretary of War under President

Martin Van Buren and was appointed as the first U.S. Ambassador to Mexico. He also was the co-founder of the National Institute for the Promotion of Science and the Useful Arts (now the Smithsonian Institute). Yeah, he did all that. But what is he best known for? Well, look at his name and see if you can figure it out. Yep! Joel Poinsett is the very person we can blame, or thank, for that ubiquitous Christmas decoration, the Poinsettia plant.

The poinsettia was named for Joel Poinsett.
Courtesy of the city of Greenville.

Poinsett had a passion for plants. He was an amateur botanist who maintained hothouses on his Greenville plantation. During his time as ambassador in Mexico, he routinely scoured the countryside for unknown plants. On one such excursion, he discovered a beautiful plant with bright red blooms. The plant he found was called cuetlaxochitl by the ancient Aztec who prized it both for its beauty and its practical uses. The Aztec extracted a purplish dye from the plant to use in textiles and cosmetics. Its milky white sap also was used to treat fever.

Strange Statues

When he returned to South Carolina, Poinsett brought cuttings of the plant and began propagating it, giving it out to friends and to botanical gardens. Its popularity grew and somewhere along the line, in about 1836, it became known as the Poinsettia.

Greenville's bronze sculpture of Poinsett, of course, is to honor him for all his accomplishments. It's located on Court Street where, on July 4, 1851, Poinsett delivered an historic speech on behalf of preserving the Union.

READING GIRL • CAMDEN

There's a 380-pound girl reading inside the Kershaw County Library. OK, so she's got a good reason for weighing that much. She's made of bronze. The statue was commissioned to make a dramatic statement on the importance of children reading.

Located at 632 West DeKalb Street.

A statue in the Kershaw County Library shows children the importance of reading.
Courtesy of the Kershaw County Library.

CHARLES TOWNES • GREENVILLE

From the surprised look on Charles Townes's face, you might think one of Greenville's Main Street mice just scampered over his foot. Not so! The expression on the statue's face recreates the surprise the Nobel Prize winner felt when the breakthrough formula that led to the invention of the laser suddenly occurred to him.

At the time, Townes, a scientist who had worked with microwaves for many years, was serving as chairman of a national committee charged with shortening wavelengths. He and the committee had worked for more than a year without answers. One sunny morning, Townes awoke and walked to Franklin Park in Washington, D.C. As he sat on a bench, an equation suddenly came into his mind. He grabbed a pen and wrote the equation on an envelope he had in his pocket.

Despite opposition from the committee, Townes and his assistant worked on the formula for three months. And finally, one day the assistant informed Townes the formula was working. Laser technology was born.

For his discovery, Townes shared in the 1964 Nobel Prize for physics. His statue sits on a bench in the very park where his serendipitous formula came to mind.

Located on the south end of Main Street.

Strange Statues

There's a hairy creature inhabiting the forests and swamps of South Carolina, and no, it's not your Uncle Buddy off on a toot. Might be Aunt Thelma, though. This creature is about seven feet tall, is sheepdog hairy, and has a face that would stop a clock. Got big feet, too. Wears about a size 52. Yep, that's Auntie T, all right.

All (well, most) kidding aside, that tall, dark, and hairy guy that many people think inhabits only the far away Pacific Northwest is quite a popular feller around the South. He's made so many appearances, in fact, that quite a few groups have formed to record and document sightings. The Gulf Coast BigFoot Research Organization is one of the premier such groups. The group maintains a database of Big Foot sightings across the Southeast. Below you'll find just a smattering of the sightings they've recorded in South Carolina. Seen a hairy Aunt Thelma wandering the woods around your house?

Natural and Manmade Wonders

Wackiness abounds on the byways of our Strange But True South Carolina. No sappy theme parks here. Instead there's a weird hodgepodge of natural and manmade wonders.

ACE BASIN • BEAUFORT

The ACE River Basin, the place where the Ashepoo, Combahee, and Edisto Rivers converge, is the largest estuary on the East Coast. Just in case you're not up on your environmental terms, an estuary is a place where river water mixes with seawater, forming a complex, always-changing environment filled with a plethora of plant and animal life.

Known as the Pearl of the Lowcountry, the ACE Basin forms a complex network of ecosystems that includes pine forests, bottomland hardwoods, barrier beaches, salt and fresh water marshes, and dense cypress swamps. Encompassing 750,000 acres, it's one of the country's largest undeveloped estuaries.

The place is teeming with life. The combination of low and high marshland, low-lying islands, and the many waterways provides a perfect environment for snakes, alligators, dolphins, otters, mink, raccoon, bob cats, deer, osprey, and other bird life. In the 1980s, the ACE Basin played a critical role in the recovery of the American bald eagle and the wood stork. With the help of biologists, both species have made a remarkable comeback.

The basin once was home to many of South Carolina's rice fields, an industry that brought much wealth to the state. Many of the fields have been replanted and now serve as a feeding ground for migratory water fowl. A variety of land and boat tours are available in the ACE Basin.

ALLIGATOR ADVENTURE • MYRTLE BEACH

This Strange But True park's got everything for everybody. You can get up close and personal with all sorts of slithery things during the park's guided tours through the swamps and marshes.

The park numbers among its denizens dozens of lizards. If you're a turtle lover, boy have they got some turtles for you! The Galapagos turtles may weigh four hundred fifty pounds, but they're just big puppies in shells, say their keepers. Then there's Bonnie and Clyde, the two bears. Raised in captivity, they are gentle and have developed human-like qualities—like refraining from eating humans, maybe?

By far the park's cuddliest residents are Boo and Sam, two cute little river otters that were bottle-raised at the park. They're just so adorable and playful that watching them, you just can't help but say, "awwww."

The main attraction of Alligator Adventure is, of course, the bevy of not-so-cuddly alligators. There are some eight hundred of the toothsome creatures lounging in pools around the park.

From April through October, the park conducts live alligator shows. There's no live feeding during the winter months because gators don't eat in the cold months—see how much we learned! But, never fear, the show must go on, so instead there's live gator handling. At all times of the year you can also visit the park's most prized residents, Casper and Wendy. Rare solid white albino alligators, these two stars have their own spacious pool to swim in.

Located on U.S. Highway 17 at Barefoot Landing.

ANGEL OAK • JOHN'S ISLAND

The Angel Oak tree is a live live oak. No, we're not repeating ourselves—the tree is a Quercus virginiana, also known as a "live oak," which is a common oak variety throughout the South. This is one of the oldest and the largest. Named for its previous owners, Martha and Justis Angel, it's thought to be at least 1,400 years old. It's sixty-five feet tall, with a circumference

The circumference of the Angel Oak tree is over twenty-five feet.
Photo by J. Allen Brack.

of more than twenty-five feet. The longest limb measures eighty-nine feet and its massive canopy shades an area of 17,000 square feet.

Located at 3688 Angel Oak Road.

Atalaya Castle and Huntington Beach State Park • Murrell's Inlet

Being one of the richest men of your time has its perks, doesn't it? Especially when you inherited your fortune and don't have to do anything so mundane as work for a living.

Take, for instance, Archer Huntington, who inherited his fortune from his step-father, railroad magnate Collis Huntington. Archer declined an offer to take over Collis's railroad empire, choosing instead to pursue a life of scholarship, archeology, and philanthropy, all the better to realize his dream of bringing a little bit of old Spain to the U.S.

In 1923, Huntington married world-renowned sculptress Anna Hyatt.

Atalaya Castle was once the home of Collis and Anna Hyatt Huntingdon.
Courtesy of the South Carolina Department of Parks, Recreation, and Tourism, DiscoverSouthCarolina.com.

Proud of his wife's work, Huntington purchased 6,635 acres for their winter home, Atalaga. In designing their home, Huntington worked entirely from his memory of the Moorish architecture he saw during his travels on the Spanish Mediterranean Coast. No blueprint was ever drawn, so to complete construction, local contractor William Thomason followed Huntington around listening to his verbal instructions. This castle still stands in the park.

After Huntington's death, most of the furnishings were sent to the couple's New York home. In 1960, a 2,500 acre tract, which included Atalaya, was leased to the state of South Carolina, which established the area as a state park.

Huntington Beach State Park contains the best preserved beach in the area. The park also includes a freshwater lagoon, salt marsh, and a maritime forest. One of the world's most productive ecosystems, the park is world-renown among birdwatchers, who come here to observe the more than three hundred species that inhabit the park.

The park also offers tours in conjunction with it Coastal Exploration Program. In addition to an aquarium, tours include the opportunity to see alligators and other wildlife and to learn the history of Atalaya.

Located at 16148 Ocean Highway.

BEE CITY • COTTAGEVILLE

Well, here's a honey of an attraction. At Bee City all the residents are busy as little bees. Oh, wait. They are bees. The bees here live la dolce vita, buzzing around their hives made up like doll-house-sized city buildings. You'll find them tootling down the city's main Bee Creek Road to the Buzz-cut Barber Shop. Left on Tupelo Drive, then on to Honey Lane, where you'll find the Pig-Bee Wig-Bee Supermarket and the B-52 Airport. How sweet!

Bee City is the brain child of owner Archie Biering, a retired shipyard laborer and amateur beekeeper. Calling his town, with its one million denizens, The Sweetest Little Town in the World, Biering strives to educate the world on the plight of the endangered honeybee.

Bee City is enclosed within high walls that shield the six thousand annual visitors from the bees as they flit around doing their pollination thing. Lectures and classroom sessions are offered to school children and seniors' groups to teach them about the life and loves of the honeybee.

There's also a gift shop that sells, big surprise, honey and other bee products.

So where can you find this Strange But True attraction? None of your beeswax! Just kidding. It's at 1066 Holly Ridge Lane.

BROOKGREEN SCULPTURE GARDENS • MURRELLS INLET

Visit Brookgreen Gardens in hopes of seeing landscaped grounds, green plants, and beautiful flowers and you'll be in for a surprise. There is all that, yes. Situated within four hundred acres of the former Brookgreen rice plantation, the garden is canopied by three-hundred-year-old oaks and fans out in a delicate butterfly shape. It's gracefully landscaped and filled with beautiful and exotic plants. Typical botanical garden stuff.

But from the moment you step through the oak-shaded entrance, you'll know Brookgreen is something much more interesting than your garden-variety garden, for planted among the brilliant azaleas and dogwoods are magnificent works of art.

Greeting you there at the entrance is the first work of art, a larger-than-life piece titled *Fighting Stallions*. Sculpted by Anna

Diana of the Chase, sculpted by Anna Hyatt Huntingdon, is one of the statues found in Brookgreen Sculpture Gardens. Courtesy of Brookgreen Sculpture Gardens.

Hyatt Huntington in the 1930s, the piece is a stunning example of Huntington's ability to capture dynamic animal energy in bronze and stone. She was one of America's foremost animal sculptors and the garden contains some of her most dramatic work.

Once inside the garden, you stroll down Oak Allee, a double row of ancient oaks, strung with Spanish moss that once led to the plantation's main home. Now it wends through the garden, where sculptures of animals, people, and mythological creatures peek out at you from every nook and cranny.

Natural and Manmade Wonders

Brookgreen Gardens, founded in 1931 by Anna and Archer Huntington, was America's first sculpture gardens. Originally designed as a showplace for Anna's work, it now contains more than nine hundred sculptures by three hundred artists on fifty acres of landscaped settings, creating a spectacular blending of nature and art. Spanning the entire period of American sculpture, from the 1800s to the present, the country's foremost artists are represented.

The sculpture garden may be the heart of Brookgreen Gardens, but it's only a fraction of the attraction of Brookgreen Gardens. Contained within thousands of acres adjacent to the gardens is the Brookgreen Gardens Lowcountry History and Wildlife Preserve, which chronicles the history of the lowcountry from the days of Native Americans to the present.

Located at 1931 Brookgreen Drive.

BUSTED PLUG PLAZA • COLUMBIA

We're not really sure why Columbia chose a puppy's favorite potty place—and a busted one at that—to grace its city, but there it is in all its gigantic glory.

The busted plug, conceived and designed by local artist Blue Sky, is thirty-nine feet tall and weighs 675,000 pounds. It lists to one side and spews thousands of gallons of water from the bottom where it's "busted."

Some folks call it "brilliant" (re: city tourism officials) and others consider it a blot on the cityscape. In fact, a poll by a local television station found Columbia citizens considered the busted plug the city's biggest eyesore. But if they're hoping for a big ol' storm to pop up and blow it away, they can forget it. For safety reasons, it was built to withstand a direct hit from a tornado.

Located on Taylor Street.

Busted Plug Plaza was designed by local artist Blue Sky.
Courtesy of Blueskyart.com.

EDISTO ISLAND SERPENTARIUM • EDISTO ISLAND

Everyone knows little boys love snakes, but Ted and Heyward Clamp did more than love them. They were nuts about 'em. As kids, they wandered the forests of Orangeburg County where they were growing up, catching snakes and bringing them home as pets. They also began catching alligators. The brothers built a pen for their pets and once word got around, people began coming for miles around to see the toothy creatures, a foreshadowing of the boys' future no doubt.

The boys grew up, as little boys are wont to do. Ted became a successful local builder and Heyward, for a while, worked for a laboratory in Miami, where he extracted snake venom. Time slipped by and they both ended up settling on Edisto Island. Although their boy days were long over, they had not given up their love of snakes and other slithery things. It was a love that had scarred them. Ted had been bitten twice and Heyward, obviously the more careless of the two, had been bitten times and had lost the tip of his left index finger to the venom of a water moccasin.

Iguanas are just one species of reptile found at the Edisto Island Serpentarium.
Courtesy of Edisto Island Serpentarium.

Despite the pain inflicted, the boys continued to dream of having a place where they could keep snakes, a place where folks could come and learn and to lose their fear of—or at least gain an appreciation for—snakes. The boys, now in their fifties, finally realized that dream with the opening of their Edisto Island Serpentarium.

Opened in 1999, the Serpentarium is more than just a place with snakes. It's an educational center that teaches about snakes and their reasons for being on Earth, a place that strives to rid folks of their fear and their "the-only-good-snake-is-a-dead-snake" mentality.

There are other slithery things living in the Serpentarium. There are iguanas, turtles, and alligators. Daily tours include a series of interactive programs to educate visitors on the habitats, behaviors, natural quirks, and feeding habits of its residents. It's just what the Clamp brothers always envisioned, a place where they could share their love of all things slithery.

Located at 1374 State Highway 174.

FOLLY ISLAND AND FOLLY BEACH • CHARLESTON COUNTY

A barrier island, Folly Beach is a result of continual sand deposits from the Longshore Current, which flows onto Folly Island from the northeast. This constant ebb and flow means the Folly Beach shoreline is a dynamic thing, continuously changing shape as sediments collect and then erode with the tides.

In addition to its beachfront, Folly Island is blessed with natural dunes, plant-filled terrain, a maritime forest, and a network of swamps and estuaries. As you might guess, these areas teem with wildlife. Natural wonders abound.

Folly Beach is a nesting ground for loggerhead sea turtles that come ashore every summer to lay their eggs. The conservation program, the Folly Beach Turtle Watch Program, is charged with monitoring the turtle nests and ensuring the baby turtles are afforded the best opportunity to hatch.

Turtles aren't the only animals plying the waters of Folly Beach. Grey bottlenose dolphins also love to frolic just off the beach. Friendly and playful gray bottlenose dolphins can also often be observed just off the beach, leaping and playing for hours. Birding is popular along the beach, Folly River, and the marshes. More than 160 types of birds can be found here, making this a photographer's dream.

Natural and Manmade Wonders

Composer George Gershwin reportedly composed the hit musical *Porgy and Bess* while living on Folly Beach. The play's main characters, Porgy and Bess, are buried in the James Island Presbyterian Church graveyard.

GAY DOLPHIN GIFT COVE • MYRTLE BEACH

The Gay Dolphin Gift Cove bills itself as the Nation's Largest Gift Shop. Maybe. For sure they have plenty of kitsch for sale. There're more than 60,000 items displayed on the store's three levels—everything from T-shirts to home furnishings.

The Gay Dolphin isn't your run-of-the-mill souvenir shop. Not by any means. Scattered among the two-dollar shark's tooth earrings and sea shell art, you'll find some right unique things for the home, such as a collection of glass top tables with themed bases.

Built in a time when "gay" was just a word that meant "happy," the Gay Dolphin has been a Myrtle Beach fixture for nearly sixty years. Its garish neon sign with the flashing arrow and three marine-blue wooden dolphins balancing brightly colored balls has beckoned generations of vacationers who come to buy their cheesy souvenirs and, until recently, to climb the store's glass tower for a pelican's-eye view of Myrtle Beach.

Time has brought changes, of course, and many of the area's former attractions have fallen. But the Gay Dolphin survives, despite new insurance restrictions that forced the closing of the glass tower in 2006 and despite efforts by snooty newcomers to have the sign removed (It's just so tacky, you know!). It's still a place for cheesy souvenirs and happy dolphins.

Located at 910 North Ocean Boulevard.

GOD'S ACRE HEALING SPRINGS • BLACKVILLE

God owns real estate in Blackville. We know. The universe is God's, but this is different. There's actually a deed in the name of God Almighty in Blackville. He's the proud owner of God's Acre Healing Springs.

The history of God's Acre Healing Springs began around 1750, when Nathaniel Walker came up on a Native American bathing in the springs. Curious, he asked the guy where the waters came from. The Native American replied that the waters came from the Great Spirit and that they were healing waters. Walker traded the local tribe of Native Americans a bag of maize to give him the springs. Having no concept of ownership, the Native Americans, no doubt, felt they were making a great deal.

The springs became known for their healing powers in 1781. Following a Revolutionary War battle on nearby Windy Hill Creek, four Tories, left for dead, were found by Native Americans, who took them to the springs. The men were healed and six months later they returned to their garrison in Charleston.

The springs changed hands many times during the years until the 1900s, when the property was acquired by L.P. Boyleston. When Boyleston died on July 21, 1944, he decreed

Natural and Manmade Wonders

in his will that the springs be deeded to God Almighty, so their healing powers would be free for everyone. Cool. We just wonder who God's going to leave the land to.

Located just off State Highway 3.

HOLLYWILD ANIMAL PARK • WELLFORD

The Big Chill. Prince of Tides. Days of Thunder. The Stand. Last of the Mohicans. These are just a few of the movies whose stars live in Hollywild. But don't bring your autograph book. With no opposable thumbs, these stars can't sign it.

Hollywild Animal Park began as a run-of-the-mill farm in the 1940s. The Meeks family farm had all the normal farm animals—horses, cows, chickens, goats—and the family enjoyed tending them. Because of a love of animals, they began to expand, bringing in the wild animals that populated the rural area of Spartanburg County. Soon their menagerie included squirrels, opossums, foxes, and other animals.

The family continued to expand its collection of animals, adding species after species. Daily, curious neighbors would drop by to see what new animal had arrived. Exasperated by these drop-ins, the family began to charge an admission fee as a discouragement. This was instead interpreted as an invitation, so David and his father finally gave in and opened the place as a zoo, called "M & M." Their small zoo featured deer, swans, monkeys, tigers, lions, ducks, bears, and even an elephant.

In 1985, David and his wife took over the business and expanded. David's talent in animal training had, by this time, become well-known in Hollywood, and he was often called upon to supply animals for movies and commercials, sparking the idea for the new name: Hollywild.

The stars of Hollywild have been featured in more than sixty-five movies and numerous television commercials, brochures, and other ventures. Although countless monkeys, birds, felines, and bears have been featured, the park's biggest stars include Donna the Elephant, Alfonso the Appaloosa, Booney the Baboon, Pongo the Orangutan, and Tank, perhaps the country's only working white rhinoceros. In addition, Chewy, a magnificent lion born at Hollywild in 1991, was used by Disney Corporation as the model for *The Lion King*.

Hollywild is now home to more than five hundred animals from all over the world. Visitors are offered the opportunity for up close and personal encounters with these animals in an Outback Safari tour through the park's seventy acres. Herds of animals roam freely here, and are friendly enough to take proffered food from your hand.

Located at 2325 Hampton Road.

INDIAN SHELL RING • HILTON HEAD ISLAND

One man's garbage is another man's national treasure.

The Indian Shell Ring, located within the Sea Pines Forest Preserve, is a four-thousand-year-old garbage dump. Left by long-ago Native American residents, it consists of oyster, clam, and mussels shells and the bones of deer, raccoon, bear, and fish. All these items were tossed out the doors of nearby huts into a ring that's 150 feet in diameter. The interior of the ring remains clear.

Natural and Manmade Wonders

Experts believe the ring was built about the same time the Egyptians built the Pyramids. The tribe was semi-nomadic, wandering up and down the Savannah River according to season and arriving at Hilton Head Island in the fall of the year. They did not have bows and arrows yet, but instead, used spears for hunting. The Shell Ring builders are thought to have invented pottery in North America.

Listed on the National Register of Historic Places, the Indian Ring Shell may be the only garbage dump protected by law. It's located a short walk from the east entrance of the preserve. The trail is well marked and has been cleared to provide a view of the entire ring. The terrain here is thought to be much as it was in the days when the ring was made.

Located at 175 Greenwood Drive.

KING HAIGLAR WEATHER VANE • CAMDEN

King Haiglar was a Catawba Indian chief who was a friend of white settlers. He was often called the Patron Saint of Camden. Seems he's been looking out for—or at least over—the city for more than two hundred years.

There's a life-sized likeness of King Haigler in the form of a weather vane topping the clock tower of the B.C. Moore department store. According to town archives, this is the third clock tower for the vane. The first tower—with the King Haiglar vane perched atop—was built in 1791 at the town's market place on the corner of Bull and Market streets. That tower and marketplace were destroyed by fire in 1812.

A new marketplace was built along Broad Street in the

1820s. This time the clock tower with the King Haiglar weather vane was placed atop the city's new City Hall and Council offices, where it stood until 1885.

King Haigler, Patron Saint of Camden, watches over the city from his perch atop a clock tower.
Courtesy of Kershaw County.

As the city grew, the marketplace continued to move and grow. In 1885, a new market place was constructed and once again, a new clock tower was built, this time atop a building housing not only the City Hall but also the town's opera house.

Years slipped by and times changed. The City Hall moved to a new location. The marketplace and opera house closed down. Throughout it all, King Haigler has continued his vigil.

Located at 950 Broad Street.

LIBERTY BELL MONUMENT • COLUMBIA

Cast in France in 1950, this replica of the famously cracked Liberty Bell was presented to the United States government by six private American businesses as a symbol of the United

Natural and Manmade Wonders

States Savings Bond Independence Drive. The dimensions and tone are identical to the original Liberty Bell. It stood outside the State House until 1970, when it was moved to its present location on the State House grounds between the Brown and Hampton buildings.

Columbia has a replica of the Liberty Bell.
Courtesy of South Carolina Legislature Online.

MAGNOLIA PLANTATION • CHARLESTON

Magnolia Plantation, South Carolina's first plantation of note, was a wedding gift from Barbadian Stephen Fox to his daughter Ann and her new husband, Thomas Drayton, who were married in the 1670s. The Draytons built the original building in 1680 and at the same time began planting what is now America's oldest garden. Over the ensuing three centuries, their direct descendants have continued to live here and maintain the plantation.

Dating from 1760, the present house, the plantation's third structure, was originally located in nearby Summerville. After the plantation's second home was burned by the Yankees during

Sherman's fiery March to the Sea, the house was dismantled and brought by barge up the Ashley River to Magnolia, where it was then…hmm…re-mantled?...on the burned-out ground floor of the original site.

The Magnolia Plantation was brought to Charleston by a barge on the Ashley River.
Courtesy of Magnolia Plantation and Gardens.

The home's living and dining areas and the Victorian water tower were added in the late 1800s. The stucco-like material that covers the house, made from phosphate gravel mined from the plantation, was added after the Charleston Earthquake of 1886. Inside, the home houses an impressive collection of Early American antique furnishings.

Located at 3550 Ashley River Road.

PEARL FRYAR'S TOPIARY GARDEN • BISHOPVILLE

Back in 1984, Pearl Fryar had never heard the word "topiary." Today, he's known as one of the world's top topiary artists. And it all started with a two dollar castoff plant from the local nursery and a desire to do something different.

Fryar says that along with the two dollar plant, he got a quick lesson on trimming from the nursery owner. That one

Natural and Manmade Wonders

lesson spurred him to trim the boxwoods growing in front of his Bishopville home. He began by trimming the hedges into the numbers "145," the street address of his home. People began talking. Fryar continued to trim, filling his yard with whimsical plant sculptures and expanding to sculpt his neighbors' plants.

Soon a desire was born. Fryar decided he wanted to win the town's Yard of the Month award, which shouldn't have been much of a challenge considering his artistry. However, this was South Carolina in 1984 and Fryar is African-American. Integration was rampant by that time, yes. Still old sentiments die hard, and in most places in the South, folks "stuck to their own." The good folks of the Bishopville's garden club saw Fryar as an outsider. Those people, the people of his neighborhood, could never be expected to keep up their yards.

In striving for recognition, Fryar displayed a talent for making plants do some strange things. Not content to just trim hedges into designs, he began to coax young plants into growing unusual shapes—perhaps with all their limbs growing in one direction or twirling around an object. Preferring abstract shapes to recognizable forms, he filled his yard with corkscrews, pyramids, mushrooms, and weird shapes nature could never come up with. His specialty seems to be the fishbone pattern. It's a strange but true sight to see—a twenty-foot tree that resembles the skeleton of a fish.

Well, Fryar accomplished his desire to garner the Yard of the Month award—three times, no less. But in doing so, he also gained something he never expected. He gained recognition as an artist, he found a way to give pleasure to others, and he opened the once-tight borders of Bishopville to the world.

Today, his yard has expanded to a three-acre garden filled with odd plant sculptures. People from all over the globe come to visit, to see what Fryar's big hands have wrought. They hail him as a visionary artist and display his work in museums across the country. If you're lucky, you may find Fryar at work during your visit. He'll stop and take time to talk, to instruct, maybe. And you'll leave, perhaps, with an appreciation not only for nature and art but for the man himself.

Fryar's home is located at 145 Broad Acres Road. His gardens are at 165 Broad Acres Road.

RIPLEY'S AQUARIUM® • MYRTLE BEACH

Having trouble sleeping? Well, plan a sleepover at Ripley's Aquarium®, South Carolina's most visited attraction, where you can count sharks instead of sheep. Oh, yeah, that oughta take care of that insomnia. Yeah, right. If you didn't have it before, you will after that!

Ripley's Sleep With The Sharks® program allows groups of fifteen or

At Ripley's Aquarium, visitors can spend the night with sharks.
Copyright 2005 Ripley's Aquarium®.

Natural and Manmade Wonders

more to bring their sleeping bags and pillows and sleep in the aquarium's Dangerous Reef shark tunnel, where toothsome big fishes swim over and around inside their plexiglass home. Fortunately, the program features a number of late-night activities, such as T-shirt painting, an aquarium scavenger hunt, educational presentations, and a late-night snack, which keeps you from getting too much time for shark nightmares. It's fun for all ages.

Located at 1110 Celebrity Circle.

SOUTH OF THE BORDER • DILLON

South of the Border—which is south of the North Carolina border, by the way—is a 350-acre resort that's all things to everyone. Sleepy? There's a whole collection of motels, containing more than three hundred rooms and suites—even several honeymoon suites (how romantic!) and a one-hundred-site camping area. Hungry? Six restaurants satisfy every craving, from fast food to steak. Bored kids driving you nuts? Turn 'em loose in Pedroland, an amusement park, complete with roller coasters and bumper cars, or the Golf of Mexico (sheesh!), the world's only indoor eighteen-hole mini-golf course or one of the three video arcades. Out of gas? You can fill 'er up here in one of the three service stations.

The resort got its start in 1949, when founder Alan Schafer built a small beer stand he called the South of the Border Beer Depot. It was located south of North Carolina's dry counties. The stand proved so profitable that in 1954, Schafer added a motel and gift shop. Renaming his new resort South of the

Border, he went all out with the faux Mexican theme. On a souvenir-buying trip to Mexico, he met two Mexican boys, whom he befriended. Helping the two to immigrate, he hired them as bell hops and used them as "spokesmen" (read: mascots) for the resort. At first folks took to calling the two Pancho and Pedro, but soon they were both being called Pedro. Today all workers at the resort are called "pedros."

Schafer was the consummate kitsch marketer. Using hundreds of miles of signs and billboards, he lit a spark of interest and fanned it into an all-consuming fire of curiosity, impossible to resist. This strategy remains the mainstay of SOB's (as it's affectionately known) marketing efforts.

Signs, signs, everywhere are signs. From Baltimore to Daytona and back again, all up and down I-95, signs telling you all about Pedro, the main spokesman. The penultimate sign is the final one welcoming you into South of the Border. This million-dollar billboard is fifty-nine feet long and twenty feet high, with more than twenty-four thousand red, blue, green, and white lamps lighting up the evening sky. Oh, but that's only the beginning.

You enter by driving through the legs of the giant Pedro, almost one hundred feet tall and weighing in at seventy-seven tons. Holding a giant SOB sign, he's wearing a huge sombrero and is lit up like a Mexican Christmas tree. Once inside you could go on sensory overload. Everywhere you look there's neon. And Mexican music is blaring through powerful loud speakers. And there are giant animals everywhere, from gorillas to dinosaurs, most wearing sombreros. Oh! Oh! And you just

Natural and Manmade Wonders

gotta ride up the two-hundred-foot sombrero tower! You take the glass elevator to the top, where you can step out onto the rim of the big hat for a bird's eye view of the entire resort.

Located just off I-95 on U.S Highway 301-501.

There are three separate stories of how Stumphouse Mountain came by its unusual name.

The name may have come about from a stump where Civil War bootleggers stored their illicit products. It also may have come from Cherokee who observed a white couple who had made a home by putting a roof over the stump of a large tree. "Stumphouse," the Cherokee called it. Then there's the legend of Isaqueena, the Creek princess living among the Cherokee on the mountain. It's she for whom the local waterfall is named. Seems she had fallen in love with a local settler. When she warned the settlers of a pending attack by the Cherokee, the betrayed tribe got ticked off. They chased the princess to the edge of the falls. As her attackers were approaching, Isaqueena hid in a stump and later jumped to her death in the waters below.

STUMPHOUSE TUNNEL • CLEVELAND

Stumphouse Tunnel was part of an ambitious project to link South Carolina's railway system to those of the Midwest. The railroad was partially constructed, but the company ran out of money and construction halted in 1850. In 1852, the idea was revived and construction on a tunnel through Stumphouse

Mountain was begun. The tunnel was to burrow 5,863 feet, but in 1859, with just 4,363 feet completed, the beginning of the Civil War and a lack of funds halted the project. Although there were attempts in 1875, 1900, and 1940 to resume progress, the tunnel was never completed.

Stumphouse Tunnel sat abandoned, used as a local picnic spot, until 1941, when a Clemson A& M College professor noted that the constant fifty-degree temperature and 85 percent humidity of the tunnel made it a perfect environment for curing cheese. As a result the college's Dairy Department decided on a little experiment. They would make Bleu Cheese on campus and use the tunnel for curing it.

Unfortunately, once again war intervened. The college lost its cheese-making specialists to World War II and milk was in short supply. So the project was scuttled until after the war. In 1951, with the war over and milk once again in good supply, the project was revived.

Using the milk from Clemson's herd of Brown Swiss and Holstein cows, the department once again began making Roquefort-style Bleu Cheese at the university and curing it inside the tunnel. In 1953, 2,500 pounds were cured within the tunnel. However, because of hot weather, the cheese-making had to be suspended during the summer months. Innovations in air conditioning at the college became available and the college began to cure its cheese on the campus, abandoning its use of the tunnel by 1958. Today, Clemson University produces 43,000 pounds of its artisan Clemson Bleu Cheese.

As for Stumphouse Tunnel, it was bought by the city of Walhalla, which maintains it as a tourist attraction. Located adjacent to Isaqueena Falls on state highway 28, it makes a perfect picnic spot.

SWAMP FOX MURALS TRAIL • CLARENDON COUNTY

One of the most unusual and yet practical tourist attractions in South Carolina involves its colorful history and various buildings in Clarendon county. It's a way to highlight the state's rich history, while giving folks a reason to get to know the county.

In deciding on just which part of South Carolina's rich history to highlight, the good folks of Clarendon County settled on the American Revolution, with good reason. There were more Revolutionary War battles fought in South Carolina than any other state. Reportedly, British texts cite the South as the reason England lost the war.

One of the most celebrated figures of the American Revolution was General Francis Marion, a South Carolina native. Born in Georgetown, Marion is considered the Revolution's greatest guerrilla fighter. He began his fighting career when the Cherokee began massacring settlers. A quick study, he learned their techniques for sneak attack and for disappearing into the swamps and forests for cover, a tactic that earned him the moniker "The Swamp Fox."

Clarendon County celebrates the Swamp Fox and the exploits of the Marion Brigade in a series of murals painted on buildings in towns across the county. The fourteen murals, painted by various artists, appear on the sides of flower shops, fire stations, grocery stores, drug stores, even doctor's offices in the towns of Paxville, Turberville, Manning, and Summerton.

Throughout the year, Clarendon County holds numerous events highlighting the murals and the history of the county, including symposia on Frances Marion and other historical figures and battle reenactments.

UFO WELCOME CENTER • BOWMAN

Those of us who believe in life on other planets can rest assured. When the aliens land, they will be adequately welcomed. However, they must land in Bowman, where Jody Pendarvis, self-appointed alien ambassador, will be waiting to greet them and offer them a familiar place to rest after their long journey.

Pendarvis has the world's only UFO Welcome Center, which he built next to his trailer. The center is a forty-two-foot-wide flying-saucer-shaped building made of wood, fiberglass, and plastic. Painted silver, the building is mounted on four columns and is designed to raise and lower with motors. It's entered by a powered ramp located underneath the saucer.

Inside, the saucer is furnished with a bed, satellite television, air conditioning, toilet, and a "decontamination chamber" (read: shower). The center, which pops up over the surrounding privacy fence, has become a local tourist attraction and has garnered national attention for Pendarvis and Bowman. So far, no aliens have been welcomed, but the UFO Welcome Center isn't sitting dormant. Seems Pendarvis moves into it during the summer months, when the saucer is cooler than his trailer.

Located at 4004 Homestead Road.

Natural and Manmade Wonders

Better watch your step in our Strange But True South Carolina. You never know when the long arm of the law may reach out and nab you for breaking some of these strange but true laws!

1. Horses may not be kept in bathtubs.

2. In New Village County, it's unlawful to sing while drinking alcohol.

3. If a man promises to marry an unmarried woman, by law the marriage must take place.

4. Fortunetellers must have a special state permit.

5. When approaching an intersection in a non-horse vehicle, you must stop one hundred feet from the intersection and discharge a firearm into the air to warn horse traffic.

6. Horses are to wear pants at all times.

7. It's illegal to dance in public in Lancaster.

8. In South Carolina it's legal to beat your wife. But only on Sunday mornings and only on the courthouse steps.

9. No work may be done on Sunday.

10. In Spartanburg, it's illegal to eat watermelons in the Magnolia Street cemetery.

Strange Museums

There's a strong sense of history here, as evidenced by the large number of museums throughout the state. But you won't find works by Picasso or Monet gracing these walls. Nah. We're much more interesting than that.

AMERICAN MILITARY MUSEUM • CHARLESTON

The American Military Museum bills itself as "a one-of-a-kind-experience." Dedicated to the men and women of all military branches, it houses exhibits from every American war—running in reverse chronological order.

You'll find seventy display cases filled with uniforms, headgear, flags, medals, personal equipment, and, yes, weapons of every kind. Highlights include

- General Dwight D. Eisenhower's original star rank insignia
- An 1820 bell crown shako (That's a hat y'all). It's one of only three in existence.
- An 1872 African-American Ninth Calvary dress blue uniform from the famous Buffalo Soldiers, the first African-American troop to be organized to serve on the Western Frontier. Most came from Louisiana and Kentucky and were veterans of the Civil War. Despite extreme prejudice from both their own officers, all of whom were white, and the people of Texas, for whom

they fought, the regiment distinguished itself as one of the most effective fighting forces in the United States Army. The museum's dress uniform is believed to be the only one in the country.

- More than four hundred pieces of military headgear and six hundred military miniature and toy soldiers.

More than just a collection of artifacts glorifying war, many of the museum's pieces have been donated by the soldiers that owned them or by their families. In many cases, uniforms still exhibit the soldier's name

The American Military Museum offers displays of uniforms and headgear from every war in which America has fought.
Courtesy of the American Military Museum.

tag stitched on its pocket and sometimes you'll find a short biography of the regular GI Joe that wore it.

The museum gives us a comprehensive look at the conflicts that have shaped both our country and the world and gives us an opportunity to reflect on the courage of those who have served and sacrificed in our military.

Located at 360 Concord Street.

BMW ZENTRUM • GREER

Zentrum. It means "focal point" in German. That's exactly what this museum is—the focal point of BMW in America. It's the only BMW manufacturing plant in the United States. Also the only BMW museum, the BMW Zentrum showcases the company's mechanical marvels and brings visitors up to date on their history.

Ever wonder just what BMW stands for? Well, we're gonna tell ya anyway. It stands for Bavarian Motor Works. The company was founded in 1913 as an aircraft motor design and manufacturing company. Their first aircraft engine, produced in 1917, set an altitude record. But that was only the beginning. Throughout the twenties, the company designed and manufactured aircraft engines and set aviation records—twenty-nine of them. The company's logo, in fact, was introduced in 1920 and is based on the circular design of an aircraft propeller.

In 1923, BMW began to branch out, producing its first motorcycle, the R 32, for which the company designed a special flat-twin engine. It wasn't until 1928 that the company began its foray into automobile design and manufacture. The first car produced was the Dixi 3/15 PS. Built under the Austin license, it was essentially the same car as the Japanese Datsun. Humble beginnings, eh? In 1932, the company produced a car that was built entirely in-house. Called the BMW AM4, it was a four-cylinder with a top speed of fifty miles per hour.

The BMW Zentrum museum offers visitors a look at the company's heritage and showcases both its motorcycles,

including a number of its renowned racing cars. The museum also features an exhibit of its famous BMW Art Car Collection. The collection was begun in 1975, when French racing driver Herve

BMW Zentrum offers views of the famous BMW Art Car Collection.
Copyright BMW Manufacturing Co.

Poulain transformed his BMW 3.0 CSL racing car into a work of art before the LeMans race. He kicked off a trend, and soon famous artists from around the world—Andy Worhol, Frank Stella, and Roy Lichtenstein—were using BMWs for a canvas. Today, the collection totals fifteen, with nine countries of every continent in the world represented.

The entire collection roams from prestigious art museum to prestigious art museum—the Louvre in Paris, the Royal Academy in London, and the New York Whitney Museum of Art—where you'd pay a pretty penny to see them. But, hey, you can see some of them for free at the Zentrum, where they are rotated on a continual basis.

Located at 1400 Highway 101 South.

BEAUFORT ARSENAL MUSEUM • BEAUFORT

One of the most significant historic sites in Beaufort, the Beaufort Arsenal Museum was built in 1798 in response to a federal mandate to create a militia and a state order to build a powder magazine and a laboratory for making shot and explosives.

The gothic-style architecture made the building a stand-out in Beaufort. It was made of brick and tabby, a cement first made by Spaniards in the early 1500s. In making tabby, shells were burned to extract lime, which was then mixed with shells and sand and poured into wooden molds to made walls and pillars.

The Arsenal became the home of the Beaufort Volunteer Artillery, which was formed in 1775. The fifth oldest military unit in the country, the BVA has served in every war fought by the United States. The unit was occupying the Arsenal in 1852, at which time the BVA renovated the badly deteriorated building. It was renovated again in 1934 by the Works Progress Administration.

Today, the Beaufort Arsenal houses a museum filled with relics of war, nature, and early industry, the first of which you'll find on the building's front lawn. The two brass trophy guns were captured from the British in 1779. Seized by Union soldiers at the fall of Fort Walker in 1861, they returned to Beaufort in 1880. The museum also traces the history of South Carolina with artifacts dating from the time of Native Americans to the earliest Spanish settlements on Parris Island to successive European settlements. The artifacts continue history into the antebellum period through the Civil War. Also covered are the early twentieth-century industries that have shaped the state, including phosphate mining, truck farming, fishing, shrimping, and oystering.

Located at 713 Craven Street.

THE BERKELEY MUSEUM • MONCKS CORNER

The artifacts of the Berkeley Museum go way back. We mean waaay back—like twelve thousand years back to the time of the Ice Age, when Native Americans first occupied the land. Contained within the 5,600-square-foot facility, you'll find all manner of historical relics from every phase of South Carolina's history.

One of the most interesting exhibits is the replica of the CSS *David*. This torpedo boat was constructed during the Civil War on the grounds where Old Santee Canal Park is now located. The vessel was cigar-shaped and carried seventy pounds of explosive on the end of a spar projecting from the bow. Although she was strictly a surface boat, her low profile and the fact that she operated late at night made her almost as difficult to see as a submarine.

On October 5, 1863, the *David* made maritime history by launching the first ever torpedo attack. Commandeered by Lt. William T. Glassell of the Confederate Navy, she slipped down Charleston Harbor to attack the ironclad USS *New Ironsides*. Under the cover of a dark night, she went undetected to within fifty yards of her target. Hailed by the *Ironsides*, Glassell fired a blast from his shotgun and plunged the *David* ahead to ram the boat with her explosive spar.

Things didn't quite work out as planned. When the explosives detonated underneath the starboard quarter of the *Ironsides*, a flume of water shot up and extinguished the *David*'s boiler fires, rendering her dead in the water and stuck beneath the *Ironsides*. Thinking their ship was sinking, Glassell and all but one crewmember, who couldn't swim, abandoned ship. When the ship didn't sink, the chief engineer climbed back aboard and rebuilt the boiler fires. He was successful in freeing the ship and sailing her back up the river to safety. Her captain wasn't so lucky. Still treading water, he was captured by the crew of the *Ironsides*. Although, the *Ironsides* wasn't sunk, she did sustain substantial damage.

The *David* went on to make several more successful torpedo attacks. Her last recorded attack was on April 18, 1864. Her eventual fate is unknown, though it's thought she may have been among a number of Confederate torpedo ships captured in February 1865.

Located at 950 Stony Landing Road.

Bob Campbell Geology Museum • Clemson

This museum rocks! The Bob Campbell Geology Museum, located within the South Carolina Botanical Garden, houses an impressive array of geological wonders. You'll find such showoffs as rocks that glow in the dark—showcased by a spectacular light show. There're cases and cases of gemstones. Collections of agates and geodes. Crystals. Meteorites. Fossils. Amazing minerals.

In addition to all that, the museum is home to Clemson's

oldest tiger, Smilodon, the saber tooth tiger. The museum's specimen is the Southeast's only mounted skeleton of this ancient kitty. Mounted on a hunk of faux Winnsboro granite, South Carolina's state rock, the skeleton strikes a menacing pose reminiscent of the Clemson tiger outside the university's Death Valley Stadium.

Located at 103 Garden Trail.

CAYCE HISTORICAL MUSEUM • CAYCE

This museum chronicles the history of the first European settlement in the South Carolina Midlands. Once called the "back country," these areas of the Old Saxe Gotha, Granby, and West Columbia were first settled in the early 1700s. The museum exhibits emphasize the periods of Colonial trade, agricultural development, and transportation from the eighteenth century. There are also Native American artifacts dating from the times these tribes inhabited the lands along the Broad, Saluda, and Congaree Rivers.

The focal point of the museum is a reconstruction of the old trading post first established by James Chestnut and Joseph Kershaw in 1765 at Granby Village, an important trading market on the Congaree River. The trading post had a rich history. Seized by the British, it was used as a fort during the American Revolution.

In 1817, it was bought by the Cayce family, who used it as a private residence for nearly one hundred years. William Cayce, affectionately known as "Uncle Billy," ran a general store here near the railroad tracks in the area that was known as Cayce

Crossroads. In 1914, when the town was incorporated, local citizens decided to honor the family by naming the town Cayce.

The museum houses six rooms of exhibits and special events are held here throughout the year.

Located at 1800 12th Street.

CHARLESTON MUSEUM • CHARLESTON

Established in 1773, while Charleston was still a British colony, the Charleston Museum was this nation's first museum. Many of its original collections were destroyed in a fire in 1778 and operations were suspended during the American Revolution, but collections resumed in 1790.

The museum was first opened to the public in 1824, and by 1859, its

The Charleston Museum houses the largest collection of South Carolina exhibits.
Courtesy of the Charleston Museum.

collection was declared to be among the finest in the nation by prominent Harvard scientist Louis Aggasiz. The outbreak of that little disagreement between the North and South caused another temporary suspension, but operations resumed soon after.

The museum is now the nation's largest and oldest collection of South Carolina exhibits. Its permanent and traveling exhibits offer histories of the state and the country, with an emphasis on natural science and ornithology. Housed within the museum and its two National Historic Landmark houses, the collections introduce visitors to the rich heritage of the Lowcountry from the early settlements through the late nineteenth century.

If you're worried about keeping the kids interested, don't be. The museum offers a special exhibit just for them. Kidstory is a hands-on exhibit that brings history alive for children and helps teach them of the Lowcountry heritage and culture.

Located at 360 Meeting Street.

CLEMSON UNIVERSITY ARTHROPOD COLLECTION • CLEMSON

Ewww! Bugs! Hundreds of them! Thousands of them! Hundreds of thousands of them! It's an entomophobic's worst nightmare. Meerkats love it, though.

The Clemson University Arthropod Collection was begun in 1890. The original collection, however, was lost in a fire in 1925. The present collection, which was begun in 1925, now numbers 102,000 of the little creepy crawlers pinned to cards and identified to genus, 36,000 pinned and sorted to categories, 45,000 preserved in alcohol, and 29,000 on microscope slides.

In addition to seeing the bugs that populate and pester the world, you'll also learn all about their habits and just what their purpose is. Some of them are quite beneficial and the world wouldn't be the same without them.

To schedule a tour, call the Clemson University Visitor Center.

COLUMBIA FIRE DEPARTMENT MUSEUM • COLUMBIA

When you're hot you're hot. Those of us who've done it will tell you fighting fire is pretty simple. You just put the wet stuff on the hot stuff. The complicated part is getting to the hot stuff. You crawl into a building that's black with smoke.

Dragging your charged hose, you crawl in, around, and over all manner of unidentified immovable objects…couch? Chair? Finally, you round a corner, and there it is, an orange glowing monster that suddenly illuminates the darkness, outlining everything in silhouette. The hot stuff! Aiming, you open the nozzle and pour out the wet stuff. A loud hissing fills your head and suddenly you're once again plunged into blackness. Voila! You've just successfully fought fire.

The Columbia Fire Department is South Carolina's largest fire department, so you can bet they put a lot of wet stuff on hot stuff. The Columbia Fire Department Museum was instituted to honor the brave men and women who risk their lives daily on the job and to showcase the department's rich tradition.

Located within the department's headquarters, the museum contains a photographic history of Columbia firefighting, a Columbia firefighter memorial, and showcases filled with firefighting memorabilia, some dating from the late 1800s when the wet stuff was delivered via a bucket brigade. The museum's prized possessions are its pieces of firefighting equipment from yesteryear. You'll find an antique hose reel, a

1903 Metropolitan Steamer horse-drawn engine, and a 1929 American LaFrance engine.

Located at 1800 Laurel Street.

CRIMINAL JUSTICE HALL OF FAME • COLUMBIA

Guns! Gangsters! Moonshine stills! What more could you ask for? The South Carolina Criminal Justice Hall of Fame is dedicated to all South Carolina law enforcement officers who have given their lives in the line of duty and pays tribute to all officers of the criminal justice profession.

The exhibits include an old moonshine still, police cars, and guns, guns, and more guns. There's also an interesting exhibit on former Public Enemy No. 1 John Dillinger. From the time he was released from prison in May 1933 until he was killed on July 22, 1934, Dillinger was the country's most notorious criminal. South Carolina native Melvin Purvis, who was FBI Special-Agent-in-Charge of the Chicago office, was in charge of the scene when Dillinger was gunned down outside a movie theater. He became known as "the man who took Dillinger." Purvis, originally from Timmonsville, is buried in South Carolina. His extensive gun collection is on display at the Hall of Fame.

Located at 5400 Broad River Road.

MACAULAY MUSEUM OF DENTAL HISTORY • COLUMBIA

The Macaulay Museum of Dental History is one of South Carolina's strangest but truest museums. Collection of dental memorabilia was a life-long avocation for South Carolina dentist Dr. Neil Macaulay, who served as a dental corpsman during

World War II and who wrote that scintillating tome, *Centennial History of the South Carolina Dental Association*. Macaulay donated his collection to the Medical University of South Carolina in celebration of the country's centennial in 1976.

You'll find a dental office circa 1900 and a collection of old-timey chairs. There's also an impressive array of torture instruments. Check out that treadle-powered drill from 1871. It provided a solid rotary cutting device for removing decay. Oh, fun. You'll find every type of pick imaginable, including one particularly painful-looking one made by Paul Revere of "The British Are Coming" fame. Open wide!

Located within the Waring Historical Library of the Medical University of South Carolina at 175 Ashley Avenue.

NMPA Stock Car Hall of Fame-Joe Weatherly Museum • Darlington

"Little Joe" Weatherly was a bit of a prankster. A true Southern character, he became known as The Clown Prince of Stock Car Racing back in NASCAR's earliest days. He had a zest for life and was famous for his pedal to the metal, no holds barred racing style, which garnered him two wins at the notoriously difficult Darlington Raceway. He was killed in a crash while racing at Riverside in 1964.

It was Joe Weatherly who first proposed the institution of a stock car museum, and so it's only fitting that it be named for him. Located at the Darlington Raceway, the National Motorsports Press Association Hall of Fame-Joe Weatherly Museum is a NASCAR fan's dream pit stop, stacked to its

"Too tough to tame," is how South Carolina Darlington Raceway is known in the racing world. The track was the dream of local businessman Harold Brasington, who returned from a trip to the 1933 Indianapolis 500 with the notion that a race track for the fledgling NASCAR would be a good idea. Folks scoffed. But Brasington ignored them.

It took until 1950, but finally Brasington opened Darlington Raceway. He had planned a true oval track, but the track's landowner insisted that his fish pond not be disturbed, so the oval had to be narrowed at turns three and four, giving Darlington a challenge not offered by other racetracks. That first race on Labor Day 1950 far exceeded Brasington's expectations with more than twenty-five thousand fans watching as Driver Johnny Mantz won the first Southern 500.

More than fifty years later, that race, now known as the Mountain Dew Southern 500, is NASCAR's Super Bowl. The raceway has undergone many renovations through the years, emerging as an ultra-modern facility, but the track remains one of the toughest in the sport.

restrictor plates with racing stuff. You can gawk over classic race cars, and see all sorts of motorsports memorabilia such as the infamous restrictor plate and the Hemi engine, photographs and an in-depth history of racing. Anything to do with racing or race car drivers is fair game. You'll find Weatherly racing shoes and a pair of Fonty Flock's Bermuda shorts. There's even a fifty-five-pound rock fish caught by driver Tiny Lund in 1963.

The rear of the building is reserved for the NMPA Hall of Fame, which features photographs, memorabilia, and interactive exhibits on NASCAR and its elite—Alan Kulwicki, David Pearson, Richard Petty, and Neil Bonnett, just to name a few.

Located 1301 Harry Byrd Highway.

REGIONAL MUSEUM OF HISTORY • SPARTANBURG

This museum is eclectic. Or is that eccentric? Its permanent collections run the gamut of topics pertaining to Spartanburg history. One of the oldest, and most curious, exhibits is the Pardo Stone. Seems that way back in 1567, Spanish explorer Juan Pardo and 250 men came to the newly established Fort Elena on Parris Island. He hadn't been there long when he and half his men were sent on a mission to establish friendly relations with Native Americans inhabiting the country's interior and to find an overland route to Mexico—to better plunder the wealth of Central America.

Experts believe Pardo's exploratory route took him through Spartanburg County, where he left a peculiar artifact. The Pardo Stone is an etched stone, perhaps akin to the Rosetta Stone. Plowed up by a farmer in 1935, the large stone is believed to have been etched by Pardo.

Perhaps one of the weirdest exhibits is the Nestle Permanent Wave machine. Looking remarkably like something from the Spanish Inquisition, the machine was invented in 1905 by German hairdresser Karl Nestle. It consisted of twelve metal rods, heated by electricity and suspended above the head. An alkali solution was applied to the hair, which was then spiraled around the rod. The woman would sit for an extended amount of time while the hair was cooked at 212 degrees. The entire process took about six hours. Nestle's wife must've loved her hubby a lot. She served as his guinea pig and had her hair completely burned off and suffered burns to the scalp—not once, but twice—when he was trying to perfect the machine!

Located at 100 East Main Street.

RICE MUSEUM • GEORGETOWN

Rice, a food staple of many countries for more than 6,500 years, arrived in the United States in 1685. A ship sailing from Madagascar was badly damaged in a storm. It landed in Charles Towne (now Charleston) and was repaired by colonists. In gratitude for their help, the ship's captain presented the colonists with some rice seeds from his cargo. Called Golden Seede Rice because of its distinctive color before cooking, it marked the beginning of the nation's rice cultivation.

Land conditions in South Carolina and Georgia, where the soil is rich and fertile and low-lying marshes are bordered by tidal fresh water rivers, made these areas ideal for rice cultivation. Production was greatly enhanced by the influx of slaves from an area in Africa that had cultivated rice for thousands of years. These slaves not only provided cheap labor that made rice so profitable, but they also provided knowledge on cultivation.

Rice soon became a major cash crop for South Carolina,

with more than three hundred tons of rice being shipped to England annually. American rice was known as Carolina Gold, which eventually became the standard for high-quality rice in the world. By 1700 so much rice was being exported from South Carolina there weren't enough ships to carry it.

The rice boom lasted until the Civil War, then it crashed hugely. Once the war was over, the high cost of labor, combined with the devastation of the war and from hurricanes, drastically reduced the profitability of rice. The rice industry floundered until the advent of the Machine Age. Unfortunately for South Carolina, the soft marshlands could not support heavy machinery. At this time, rice production moved into states where machines could be used. Today, the United States is once again a major rice producer. South Carolina, however, despite its nickname as the Rice State, no longer produces rice for export.

Georgetown's Rice Museum uses dioramas, maps, artifacts, and other exhibits to educate visitors on the history of those bygone days. It's located in the 1842 Old Market Building beneath the Town Clock. The hour-long tour also includes a tour of the Kaminski Hardware Building, also built in 1842, which houses the Maritime Museum Gallery.

SLAVE RELIC MUSEUM • WALTERBORO

Yes, this museum is quite Strange But True. It's also disturbing. And powerful. The purpose of the Slave Relic Museum is to preserve, document, and celebrate the history and culture of the people of African descent. It's an expansive mission for a small museum, but it's a mission accomplished.

Strange Museums

Despite being enslaved, Africans in America were active in creating their own history and culture, and although many of the museum's exhibits are upsetting, many others are uplifting. They provide a glimpse into the ingenuity and spiritual grace of a people so long oppressed.

One of the most upsetting exhibits, no doubt, is the collection of chains, ankle shackles, and neck collars, most notably the child's neck collar. When viewing these items, one can only guess at the horror these instruments engendered. At the same time, one can't help but wonder at the beauty of the intricate designs on some of the collars, designs created by a slave who was a Charleston plantation blacksmith.

Side by side with these and other instruments of slavery, you'll find beautiful examples of slave-made artistry. In one exhibition case, you'll find a branding iron and a whip next to a handmade doll. In the room set up as a replica of an 1820s slave cabin, there's a handmade bed and cradle along with chains and shackles resting on the fireplace. There are also advertisements for the sale of slaves and notices of runaway slaves, such as the one who had "his left eye out, some scars from a dirk on and under his left arm, and much scarred from a whip."

Museum owner and curator Danny Drain says these items are juxtaposed in an effort to understand both sides of the story. One of his main interests is understanding the mindset of a person that would allow him to enslave another human.

The Slave Relic Museum is located on the first floor of Drain's antebellum home at 208 Carn Street.

SOUTH CAROLINA COTTON MUSEUM • BISHOPVILLE

The South Carolina Cotton Museum preserves a time when cotton was king of the South. You'll find original farm equipment showcased in interactive displays in authentic settings. There's a replica of an old-time "shotgun" house, so named because of its unusual construction. Shotgun houses were long narrow houses, one room wide and two to three rooms long, with either side opening into the hallway. The name comes because you could stand at

"Model of the Boll Weevil" is one of the exhibits found within the South Carolina Cotton Museum.
Courtesy of South Carolina Cotton Museum.

the front door and shoot a shotgun straight through to the back door without hitting anything. They were built by and for farm tenants and sharecroppers in the late 1800s to the mid-1900s.

You'll also find unique cotton products and interpretive programs that entertain and educate. A favorite is a kid-oriented program titled "From Seed to Shirt," that describes how a cotton seed ends up as the shirt on your back.

Located at 121 West Cedar Lane.

Strange Museums

SOUTH CAROLINA RAILROAD MUSEUM • WINNSBORO

The sound of a train whistle has a profound effect on us humans. Echoing through a moonless night, it pierces the soul with a lonesome cry and makes us long for faraway places we'll never see, smiling faces we'll never meet. Whooooo! Whoooo! You can just hear it now, can't you?

At the South Carolina Railroad Museum, you can hear that lonesome whistle blow. And ride the rails. Don't expect to see many faraway places, though. It's just a ten-mile ride along the old Rockton and Rion Railroad line, which runs westward through the Rion community.

The museum also has a large collection of railroad equipment to see. There are passenger cars, freight cars, Pullmans, cabooses, and the museum's prized possession, a steam engine. Spend the afternoon steeped in railroad lore and listening to the echo of the train whistle. And maybe somewhere in the far distance, you can hear the sound of a lonesome voice singing, "I hear that train a'comin'. It's comin' round the bend."

Located at 110 Industrial Park Road.

SOUTH CAROLINA STATE MUSEUM • COLUMBIA

Founded in 1973 and housed in the historic Columbia Mill textile building, the South Carolina State Museum presents "the essence and diversity of South Carolina." It provides a comprehensive cross section of the state's history in four floors of spectacular exhibits on natural and cultural history, art, and science and technology. Called "the museum that sits within the largest artifact," the former mill was the world's first totally electric textile mill when it opened in 1894.

The South Carolina State Museum is located in the historic Columbia Mill textile building.
Courtesy of the South Carolina State Museum.

Located at 301 Gervais Street.

SOUTH CAROLINA TOBACCO MUSEUM • MULLINS

Thank you for smoking! Since colonial times, tobacco has been an important crop in South Carolina. English settlers arriving from Barbados brought golden leaf tobacco seeds with them and immediately began cultivating them, a lack of manpower being the only holdback in a larger production. To remedy that, the fledgling colony offered free land to anyone agreeing to come live and cultivate tobacco.

Plantations spread across the state and for the next two hundred years golden leaf tobacco crops prospered, alongside rice and indigo. That is, until the Civil War, which devastated all South Carolina agriculture, including tobacco. After the war, agriculture experienced a decline as the development of the textile industry emerged in South Carolina.

Strange Museums

Life wasn't over for tobacco in South Carolina, however. The introduction of the new bright leaf variety, so called because of its bright lemon color during curing, brought a rally for tobacco production throughout the sandy coastal plains at the end of the nineteenth century. The development of this new variety was pioneered in 1894 by W.H. (Buck) Daniel in the northeast Pee Dee area. Daniel founded the first tobacco warehouse in Mullins, a supply store, a redrying plant, and the Bank of Mullins.

Mullins, in fact, is the town that tobacco made. By 1895, more than two hundred tobacco barns had sprung up in Mullins, and the town became the state's largest tobacco market. It soon became known as the Tobacco Capital of South Carolina. The increased demand for bright leaf tobacco spurred increased production in South Carolina, with calls by officials for farmers to abandon cotton for tobacco. By 1900, South Carolina ranked sixth among the tobacco growing states, up from nineteenth.

Although that big tobacco boom didn't last, tobacco remains a staple for South Carolina—and Mullins—agriculture. Tobacco barns can still be found around the Pee Dee area, where bright leaf growers produce some of the highest quality tobacco in the nation, and tobacco remains an important part of South Carolina's economy. No other crop, in fact, brings a higher profit per acre.

Located inside the historic train depot in downtown Mullins, the South Carolina Tobacco Museum pays tribute to tobacco and rural farm life prior to 1950. You'll find exhibits showing the complete growing cycle from seed to auction. There are all types of tobacco equipment, a barn, and blacksmith tools. A multi-media library includes a fifteen-minute DVD titled *When Tobacco Was King*, which explores the relationship between tobacco and Mullins for the last 110 years.

Located at the intersection of Northeast Front and Main street.

The Best Friend of Charleston, so dubbed by Charleston merchants who saw it as their economic savior, was the first steam engine in the United States to establish regularly scheduled passenger service. Making its debut run on Christmas Day 1830, it did indeed return economic prosperity to Charleston and establish the railroad system in South Carolina.

The life of the *Best Friend* was short, however. Tragedy struck after only a few months. A careless fireman caused an explosion that killed him and blew the *Best Friend* to smithereens. Luckily, by that time another engine was already established and the accident was only a minor setback to railroading in Charleston. Within three years, the railroad company had a fleet of six engines running through Charleston, a fleet that included *The Phoenix*, an engine built from the remains of the *Best Friend*.

In its short life the *Best Friend* not only returned prosperity to Charleston, it also revolutionized American transportation. To honor that feat and commemorate the one hundredth anniversary of the South Carolina Canal and Railroad Company, a replica of the *Best Friend* was constructed in 1928 using the original plans. It was donated to the City of Charleston in 1993 and is currently on display at Engine House 31 on Ann Street in Charleston.

The Haunting of South Carolina

Mist rising on moonlit nights. Ghostly apparitions floating through hallowed halls. Strange and scary noises. South Carolina can be a spooky place at night. With a past so rich in history, it's no wonder there are haints wandering this land. Here's just a smattering of South Carolina's legendary ghost tales.

1843 BATTERY CARRIAGE HOUSE INN • CHARLESTON

The 1843 Battery Carriage House Inn is one of the most haunted houses in one of the country's most haunted cities. Guests of the 1843 Battery Carriage House Inn have reported so many ghostly encounters, in fact, the owners have started recording them. So far, they report, the encounters center around two entities known as the "headless torso" and the "gentleman ghost."

No one is quite sure who—or what—the headless torso is. The owners say it's a misnomer to call it headless. They believe he does, indeed, have a head. It's just usually shrouded in darkness so the spirit is perceived as headless. Judging from the clothing he wears and considering that the house was built in 1843, they speculate that he's a soldier from the Civil War. An unfriendly spirit as well, he's been seen only in Room Eight.

The Haunting of South Carolina

An incident involving the headless torso happened to a man named Paul, who was staying with his wife in Room Eight. Ensconced in the antique bed, he was sleeping on his side, facing the wall. He suddenly became aware of a sensation of being watched. He was still asleep, he said, but what was happening was too real to be a dream.

He said he could see someone standing next to the bed, and since the antique bed was higher than normal, what he could see without raising his head was just the torso of a very large, barrel-chested man. If there was a head, it was shrouded in darkness. The same with the feet and legs. The apparition wore several layers of clothing, with the top layer being some type of outer wear with no buttons—a cape perhaps. This outer garment was made of a type of rough material. When Paul reached out to feel it, rubbing it between his thumb and forefinger, it felt rough and scratchy, like burlap. It was this sensation of touch, he said, that helped to convince him this was more than a dream. That, and the fact that he could hear raspy breathing, as if the apparition were suffering from allergies.

When Paul touched the coat, the breathing deepened into a threatening moan, as if the apparition were warning him that he didn't want to be touched. At this point, he experienced a feeling of fear, as if the apparition were about to do some harm to him. He tried to scream but was unable to. He kept struggling and finally croaked out a small sound, which brought him to full consciousness. The apparition was gone.

Although he admits to being asleep throughout the incident, Paul was convinced it was more than a dream. The apparition, he said, was a tough customer, someone he wouldn't want to meet in an alley on a dark night. Or in a quiet bedroom on a dark night.

The gentleman ghost that inhabits the inn's Room Ten is much different. One encounter with him was described by a set of twin sisters identified as DC and DS, who stayed in that room on May 19, 1992. When the sisters retired for the evening, DC placed a chair in front of the door, telling her sister that it would serve as a barrier against intruders.

The sisters were sleeping in the same bed, with DC on the left side and DS on the right, facing the door. DC fell asleep almost immediately, but DS was restless, and she lay staring at the doorway. Suddenly, she noticed a wispy gray apparition floating through the door. No facial features were visible and she was unable to discern any clothing, but she was sure it was the figure of a slightly-built man, about 5'8" tall.

As she watched him, he glided in an upright position over to the bed and lay down in the small space between her and the edge of the bed. He placed his right arm over her shoulders. She didn't feel the pressure of his arm. Neither did she feel frightened or threatened.

Wishing to share the experience with her sister, she quietly called her name. When DC spoke up to answer her, the apparition disappeared. She was disappointed that he had left and speculated that he was disturbed by the renovations of the house. She thought he might be looking for a quiet place to get some rest and was hoping they'd be obliged to share their bed. In a later letter to the inn's owners she expressed a wish to return someday to see if her "Gentleman Visitor" would come to call again.

The owners say they've never personally seen the ghosts that haunt their inn, but they believe their guests when they say they've experienced something otherworldly. They're intrigued by the stories, and are, no doubt, grateful that they have earned the inn its place on Charleston's ghostly tour.

THE LEGEND OF ANNABEL LEE • CHARLESTON

Annabel Lee by Edgar Allan Poe

It was many and many a year ago,
    In a kingdom by the sea,
That a maiden there lived whom you may know
    By the name of ANNABEL LEE;——
And this maiden she lived with no other thought
    Than to love and be loved by me.

I was a child and she was a child,
    In this kingdom by the sea,
But we loved with a love that was more than love—
    I and my ANNABEL LEE—
With a love that the winged seraphs of heaven
    Coveted her and me.

And this was the reason that, long ago,
    In this kingdom by the sea,

A wind blew out of a cloud by night, chilling
    My beautiful ANNABEL LEE;
So that her high-born kinsman came
    And bore her away from me,
To shut her up in a sepulchre,
    In this kingdom by the sea.

The angels, not half so happy in heaven,
    Went envying her and me—
Yes!—that was the reason (as all men know,
    In this kingdom by the sea)
That the wind came out of the cloud by night,
    Chilling and killing my ANNABEL LEE.

But our love it was stronger by far than the love
    Of those who were older than we—
    Of many far wiser than we—
And neither the angels in heaven above,
    Nor the demons down under the sea,
Can ever dissever my soul from the soul
    Of the beautiful ANNABEL LEE.

For the moon never beams, without bringing me dreams
    Of the beautiful ANNABEL LEE;
And the stars never rise, but I feel the bright eyes
    Of the beautiful ANNABEL LEE;
And so, all the night-tide, I lie down by the side
Of my darling—my darling—my life and my bride,

The Haunting of South Carolina

> In her sepulchre there by the sea,
> In her tomb by the sounding sea.

Any high school senior is, no doubt, familiar with Edgar Allan Poe's poem, "Annabel Lee." Most scholars will tell you the poem, Poe's last, was about his recently deceased wife. Most Charlestonians will tell you that's bunk. If the poem's about Poe's wife, they'll say, then why wasn't it named "Virginia," which was the name of his wife? They contend that the melancholy poem is Poe's version of the Charleston legend of Annabel Lee.

You see, according to the legend, a young woman named Annabel Lee met a young sailor on temporary assignment in Charleston, the kingdom by the sea. Theirs was a whirlwind romance. Though they hadn't known each other long, they fell deeply in love and spent every spare moment together.

Unfortunately, Annabel Lee's father was a strict man. When he caught the young lovers together one day, he flew into a rage and forbade them ever to see each other again. Ah, but young love is not so easily thwarted. The two continued to see each other on the sly. Annabel Lee would sneak out whenever she could and they would rendezvous at the nearby Unitarian Church Cemetery.

But fathers are not so easily fooled. One day he saw his daughter sneaking into the cemetery. He followed her and found her once again with the sailor. Furious, he grabbed her by the arm and dragged her back home. Locking her in her room, he vowed that this time she would obey him.

He kept such a close eye on her that she wasn't able to sneak out, or even to get a note to her brave sailor. While she was so incarcerated, the sailor was transferred to Virginia. Heartbroken, he left without seeing her again.

Many months later, he received tragic news from the kingdom by the sea. Yellow fever had struck, they told him. It was an ill wind that blew, chilling and killing his beautiful Annabel Lee. Devastated, he rushed back to Charleston to say a tearful goodbye. Her highborn kinsman (read: father) who had born her away from him, however, was a vindictive and cruel man. He refused to allow the sailor to attend his daughter's funeral and her burial in the family plot at their old meeting place, the Unitarian Church Cemetery.

His vindictiveness went even further. He ordered that the graves of her nearby relatives be dug down to three feet and then re-covered to make them look fresh and indistinguishable from Annabel Lee's. In this way, he planned to keep the sailor from knowing exactly where she was buried.

No matter. The grief-stricken sailor spent hours in the cemetery. It mattered not which was her grave. He mourned her loss, knowing she was close, and remembered the happy times he had there, laughing and loving his beautiful Annabel Lee.

According to Charleston legend, the beautiful Annabel Lee still walks among the living. Her spirit has been sighted strolling disconsolately through the Unitarian Church Cemetery. Many Charlestonians believe she walks there among the gravestones, searching for her lost sailor.

The Haunting of South Carolina

The Unitarian Church Cemetery is located at 4 Archdale Street.

DOCK STREET THEATRE • CHARLESTON

Opened in 1736, the original Dock Street Theatre was the first theatre to be built in America. It was located on the corner of Dock and Church Streets, facing Dock Street, which was later renamed Queen Street. For the next several years, the theatre was a popular Charleston attraction, featuring plays and operas. Although its true fate is unknown, it's thought to have been burned in 1740, when a huge fire devoured the city's historic French section.

The original Dock Street was America's first theatre.
Courtesy of Dock Street Theatre,
www.charlestonstage.com.

In 1809, several buildings on the Church Street side were renovated and the Planter's Hotel was opened on the site. Offering superior lodging, excellent food, and innovative drinks—it's the home of the Planter's Punch, a tasty and fruity little rum concoction—the hotel became popular with planters from middle South Carolina.

In 1835, the hotel was remodeled, with the addition of a wrought iron balcony. The silhouette of that balcony against the spire of St. Philip's Episcopal Church has become one of the most photographed images in the city. For fifty years, the hotel was the principal hotel in Charleston, popular with plantation owners and seafaring merchants alike.

After the Civil War, the Planter's Hotel went out of business and fell into disrepair. It was certain to simply disintegrate there on its foundation, but in 1930, the building became a Works Progress Administration project. It was restored, renovated, and reopened. It was taken over by the city of Charleston and was once again named the Dock Street Theatre, even though Dock Street had long since been named Queen Street. Today the Dock Street Theatre is home to the Charleston Stage Company, a community performing group. It also houses Charleston's Cultural Affairs office and the City Gallery, an exhibition venue for local artists.

Located at 135 Church Street.

GAUCHE, THE JESTER HUGUENOT • BEAUFORT

Beaufort's got a little ghost story for ya. According to legend, the story began back in 1562. That year, French Naval officer Jean Ribaut was sent to America with a group of 150 Huguenots to found a colony. He took the scenic route, but eventually wound up in Port Royal Sound, where he established Charlesfort on what is now Parris Island.

Among Ribaut's colonists was a dwarf named Gauche. A jester by trade, Gauche often wore a costume—pointed three-corner hat, brightly patterned coat and pants, and little pointed shoes with bells on the toes. According to reports, Gauche compensated for his size by being a tough customer.

Things didn't work out well for the colony. There was a fire early on that destroyed most of their supplies, and although Ribaut had returned to France to bring more supplies, circumstances prevented his return. With colonists dying right and left, the survivors enlisted the help of the Orista Indians to build a ship to return to France.

The return trip was no picnic. The colonists' meager supplies ran out quickly and they soon found themselves dining on leather shoes and jackets. According to legend, when those delectable treats ran out, the desperate sailors drew lots and dined on the loser before being rescued by an English ship.

The exact fate of Gauche is not known. Some say he died of illness at Charlesfort and, Lord knows, what with the heat, the humidity, and all those bloodthirsty mosquitoes, there was a lot of that going around. Some say he was hanged by a Captain Albert, who must've taken umbrage at one of the jester's pranks. Still others say the dwarf turned out to be the loser of the food lottery aboard the ill-fated return ship—although he would've made a small meal, we'd think.

Whatever his actual fate, the general consensus is that Gauche now resides in one of Beaufort's most beautiful homes. Often called the Castle because of the medieval feel of its architecture, the Joseph Johnson House was built in 1861 by Dr. Joseph Fickling Johnson. It's said to be an exact replica of a house in England, subsequently destroyed in World War II.

Soon after the Johnson house was completed in 1861, reports began to surface of a peculiar ghost that lived in the cellar. Gardeners reported seeing a dwarf dressed in jester's clothing wandering the grounds. They would often catch just a glimpse of him as he rounded a corner of the house.

Even Dr. Johnson reported seeing the apparition one night. He said he saw a face peeking through the window at him and when sighted it scurried away, laughing hysterically, with the bells on his shoes tinkling a mad tune. Johnson's little daughter, Lily, reported that Gauche would join her in the tea parties she held in the basement of the house. She said he swore a lot. He also liked to play his jester's pranks on houseguests, moving furniture and slamming doors all night along, the sounds of which were always accompanied by the sound of the tinkling bells on his feet. He's also been known to leave red handprints on upstairs windows.

According to Lily, who, in later life, reported on her experiences, the family discovered that Gauche was communicating by a code tapped out on tables. They found someone who could translate and learned that he was speaking in archaic sixteenth-century French. A report about a houseguest who interviewed the malevolent Gauche was published in *Tales of Beaufort* by Nell S. Graydon. In the interview the houseguest asked the spirit his name, to which he replied "Gauche." He said he lived in the cellar of the house because it reminded him of his childhood home. The guest then asked if she could see him, to which he puckishly replied, "No, I do not show myself to fools."

The Haunting of South Carolina

There is another popular story about Gauche, who would seem to be a hungry, wandering spirit. According to legend, in 1969, he wandered across town to the Howard Danner home and stole a roast that Mrs. Danner had left sitting on the stove. The police report speculated that Gauche the ghost had become hungry and had absconded with the roast.

If so, he must've enjoyed it so much that he visited the home of a neighbor the very next night and stole that family's roast dinner, as well. The house, which had been locked, looked undisturbed, except for the missing roast.

Uh huh. Anyway, should you visit the Joseph Johnson House at 411 Craven Street, you might just get a glimpse of the jester's ghost. That is if he doesn't think you a fool.

GRAY MAN • PAWLEYS ISLAND

The Gray Man of Pawleys Island is one of South Carolina's oldest and most famous ghost stories. For more than one hundred years, this ghost, a dapper man dressed in a gray suit, has appeared to area residents to warn them of coming hurricanes. As the legend goes, he's appeared before every major hurricane to hit Pawleys Island. He warns the person to whom he has appeared that he should pack up his family and leave the island. If the person heeds the warning, it's said, his home is spared by the hurricane.

There are several versions of the story and no one knows for sure just who the Gray Man was in real life. One of the most enduring stories claims that the Gray Man is the spirit of Plowden Charles Jeannerette Weston, the owner of Hagley

Plantation. Weston was a favored son of a wealthy rice plantation baron in Georgetown. He was reared at Laurel Hill Plantation, where his parents doted on him.

Despite the fact that his father was staunchly anti-British, he wanted his son to have a proper British education. In his younger years, Weston was privately educated by a British tutor. Then at the age of twelve, his whole family temporarily moved to England so that he could be educated there. The family eventually returned to South Carolina, but Weston stayed on in England to finish his education at Cambridge. It was there that he met and fell in love with Emily Frances Esdaile, the beautiful daughter of an English baronet.

Weston feared his father would not approve of the union because of his anti-British bias. He was, however, pleasantly surprised when his father reluctantly gave his blessing. According to legend, the elder Weston, bent on a little one-upmanship, kicked off a competition to see which father would be the most generous. When Emily's father gave the couple a dowry of seven thousand pounds, Plowden's dad arrogantly endowed them with seventy thousand pounds, a house in London, a house in Geneva, and Hagley Plantation in Georgetown. Contest over. Even an English baronet couldn't compete with that kind of wealth.

Plowden and Emily married in August 1847 and settled into Hagley Plantation, with its vast and fertile fields of rice extending from the cypress-lined Waccamaw River to the blue Atlantic. Like many lowcountry planters eager to escape the humid summer with its malaria-bearing mosquitoes, Plowden and Emily built a summer home on Pawleys Island, and the couple spent a blissful decade together, dividing their time between Hagley and their beautiful home on Pawleys Island.

By the late 1850s, however, the growing dissension between the North and South began to splinter their peaceful existence. Plowden, a published historian and fiery orator, gave many speeches and published articles warning of the coming war. As a plantation and slave owner, he supported the Southern cause. When the war began, he served as the company commander of the Georgetown Rifle Guard, personally outfitting the 150 men in his charge. During the early part of the war, he and Emily frequently entertained the regiment and their ladies at his Pawley's Island home.

Near the end of the war, Plowden contracted tuberculosis. His friends in the state legislature, knowing he wouldn't give up his command without a good reason, engineered his election to lieutenant governor of South Carolina. He accepted the position, but was unable to serve for long, for the tuberculosis worsened and, by January 1864, he lay dying in Conway, South Carolina.

At Plowden's request, Hagley's servants were brought to Conway, where they each received a gift to thank them for their years of service. His last moments were spent with Emily. After his death, his body was transported by canoe down the Waccamaw River to Hagley. He was buried next to his father in the churchyard of the All Saints' Waccamaw Episcopal Church, where he and Emily were married.

Because of Plowden Weston's devotion to his Pawleys Island home—now the Pelican Inn, a luxurious bed and breakfast—

many people believe it is he who wanders the beach dressed in gray. In life, they say, he warned his friends and neighbors of the perils of a coming war. In death, he warns of the dangers of impending storms.

HEADLESS HORSEMAN • CAMDEN

The Battle of Hobkirk Hill was an important battle of the American Revolution. In 1871, it seems that Camden was a key British base, one the colonists very much wanted to obtain. To achieve that goal, American Major General Nathanial Greene was sent with a contingent of 1,500 to capture it. They were camped on Hobkirk Hill on April 25, 1781, when British General Lord Francis Rawdon staged a surprise attack. Greene was caught by surprise, but the discipline he had drilled into his men proved valuable. He was able to quickly muster a force of 930 into battle and defend his position.

The battle was fierce and the Americans fought valiantly. According to legend, during the heat of battle, an American soldier was charging through the battlefield on his trusty steed, when a cannonball sailed through the air and hit him, severing his head from his body.

The soldier's horse was unharmed, and it charged off with the soldier still in the saddle, disappearing into the swamp near Black River Road. The battle raged on and, despite their valiant effort, the Americans were forced to retreat. It wasn't a complete defeat, however. The damage they inflicted upon the British resulted in their subsequent abandonment of Camden, a vital move that helped the Continentals to eventually take South Carolina.

The Haunting of South Carolina

Not long after the battle, reports began circulating around Camden about a strange apparition haunting the battlefield. The apparition was that of a soldier mounted on a charging horse. Just your everyday ghost story. Except for one thing. This horseman has no head. Legend has it that the headless horseman can be seen on foggy nights, especially when the moon is full. He wanders the battlefield—searching for his head no doubt. He disappears before daylight.

Interestingly enough, the story has a real basis in fact, for historians agree that such an incident did occur during the Battle of Hobkirk Hill. They're not sure, however, if it was an American or a British soldier that lost his head. Doesn't matter. It's a great campfire story. Shh! What's that? Sounds like hoofbeats....

THE HERMITAGE • MURRELLS INLET

This is the story of young Alice Flagg, a woman who believed in love. Hers is a story of tragedy and a story of love denied.

The year was 1849 and Alice and her mother had come to Murrell's Inlet to live with Alice's older brother, Dr. Allard Flagg, at the summer home he had just built. As the seashore home of the owner of the Wachesaw Plantation, the Hermitage was a beautiful showplace where Allard Flagg wined and dined the elite of South Carolina society. Social status and prestige were the lifeblood of Alice's family. Only the most important people were invited to their gay soirees and only someone who would be an asset to their place in society could ever be considered as marriage material.

Already Alice's brothers had set their sights on the Ward sisters—Penelope for Allard and Georgianna for Arthur. The Wards of Brookgreen Plantation were the most noted of the planter families of the 1840s. On their plantation they produced millions of pounds of rice and other vegetables. And they diversified as well, with a salt-making system capable of producing forty bushels of salt daily. Ah, yes, the Ward sisters were indeed a suitable match for the Flagg boys.

Fifteen-year-old Alice, however, didn't consider social status a prerequisite for marriage. Love was all that mattered to her. And this would prove to be her undoing. You see, Alice had fallen in love with a working man. By some accounts, the young man was a turpentine merchant; by others, a lumberman. Regardless, he was considered quite unsuitable by Alice's family.

The first time her beau came to call, he was met at the door by Allard, who, instantly judging him unworthy, sent him packing. Alice was outraged. She continued to see him secretly and after several weeks had passed, again invited him to the Hermitage. They planned that the young man would arrive in his carriage and take Alice for a buggy ride.

This time she was watching for him and when he arrived, she was out the door and into the carriage before Allard could stop her. Her brother, however, caught them before they could leave and grabbed the young man by the arm. Forcing him out of the buggy, he gave him his own horse to ride and jumped into the buggy beside Alice. The ride, of course, was an uncomfortable affair, with the man riding beside the carriage.

The Haunting of South Carolina

Despite the discomfort, Alice was in a state of bliss, for the young man had proposed and had presented her with a modest engagement ring. At a family meeting following the man's departure, Allard noticed the ring and flew into a rage. He demanded that she return the ring, which she agreed to do. However, she merely removed it and wore it hidden from view on a ribbon around her neck.

Alarmed by the state of affairs, Alice's family decided they had to put a stop to this budding romance. Alice, it was decided, would be sent to school in Charleston, a move they carried out immediately.

Alice was very unhappy in Charleston. Missing her beau, she spent her days and nights sequestered in her tiny room, crying and fingering the ring that still hung on a ribbon around her neck. After several months, she fell quite ill. By the time Allard was notified of her sickness—malaria, perhaps—she was delirious with fever. He rushed to Charleston and, loading her into the carriage, began the long trip back to Murrell's Inlet.

Unfortunately, the four-hour trip proved too much for Alice, and by the time they reached the Hermitage, she was unconscious. She died a few days later. After her body was prepared for burial and she was lying in state in her favorite white dress, Allard discovered the engagement ring on its ribbon around her neck. Grief stricken and furious, he tore the ribbon from her neck and tossed the ring into the bay. She was then buried in the cemetery of All Saints Church, where her grave is marked by a simple stone with "Alice" carved upon it.

Bet you've guessed that's not the end of the story. According to legend, Alice still walks among the living. Soon after her death and for the 140 years following, Alice has been seen. Wearing her beautiful white gown, she's been sighted entering the great hall of the Hermitage and ascending the stairway to her old bedroom. She's also been seen wandering the cemetery grounds. Those who have seen her say she seems to be searching for something—the lost ring, no doubt.

LIGHTHOUSE • HILTON HEAD ISLAND

By all accounts, Adam Fripp took his job seriously. A dedicated lighthouse keeper, he knew it was vital that the Hilton Head Lighthouse lamps stay lit to warn sailors away from sure death on the rocky shore. He often disregarded his own safety to climb the tower to the lantern room and keep the light burning.

One night in 1898, Fripp and his twenty-one-year-old daughter, Caroline, were riding out a hurricane at the lighthouse, trying to keep the lamp lit. Fripp had made the challenging climb to the lantern room to check on the light, when a sudden, wild gust of wind shattered a glass pane and extinguished the light. At that same moment, Fripp collapsed to the floor.

Hearing the commotion, Caroline hurried up the tower to find her father in the throes of a fatal heart attack. When she tried to leave for help, he ordered her to stay and with his last breath begged her to relight the lantern and somehow keep it lit throughout the night. Caroline kept her word and despite the dangerous conditions, overwhelming odds, and the stress of knowing her father lay dead just a few feet away, she kept the lantern glowing throughout that terrible night.

Unfortunately, the stress of the night proved too much for Caroline. She died just three weeks later and was buried in a beautiful blue gown in a nearby cemetery. But, of course, that's not the end of the story.

According to legend, Caroline, dressed in her blue gown, is faithfully keeping her promise to her father. She's been seen wandering the grounds around the lighthouse and there have been numerous reports of the sound of a woman crying coming from inside the lighthouse, especially on stormy nights.

MERRIDUN INN • UNION

First a little history. Merridun, a stately antebellum mansion listed on the National Register of Historic Places, was built in 1855, by William Keenan, a wealthy local merchant and one-time mayor of the small town of Union. Known as the Keenan Plantation, the farm, at that time, consisted of four thousand acres of cultivated land.

The plantation was bought in 1876 by Union lawyer Benjamin Rice, who adjoined it to his existing plantation, creating a new eight-thousand-acre farm, growing mainly cotton. Rice, who used the Union house as his main residence, completed a major renovation in the early 1880s.

It was around this same time that Thomas C. (T.C.) Duncan came to Union to work with his grandfather, Benjamin Rice. In 1885, he married and brought his new bride, Fannie Merriman, to live with him at the plantation that he, by now, had inherited from his grandparents. He renamed it "Merridun," combining the three surnames—Merriman, Rice, and Duncan.

T.C. was an influential man, who, by 1893, had almost single-handedly restored the town of Union to the wealth and power it had enjoyed before the Civil War. Introducing the textile industry to Union, he built the town's first successful cotton mill within sight of his mansion. And that's not all. Both an industrial and political leader, he served two terms in the South Carolina House of Representatives, constructing the mill in Buffalo, Union's B.U.C. Railroad, and the hydro-electric plant.

After inheriting Merridun, T.C. completed an extensive remodel of the original manor, replacing the double piazza's plain Doric columns with Corinthian columns and adding side wing marble porticos.

Inside, the 7,900-square foot mansion contained—and still does—a stunning curved stairway, large foyers on both floors, a music room, seven bedrooms, multiple bathrooms, and a third story cupola. The carriage barn still houses T.C.'s favorite carriage. Unique architectural features added include frescoed ceilings in the music room and dining room, stenciling, and beautiful chandeliers.

The stunning mansion is now a luxury bed and breakfast inn, nestled among shady oaks and magnolias. And by all accounts, The Inn at Merridun is quite a spirited place. According to legend, as many as ten different ghosts frequent the inn. First, there's T.C. and Fannie, who seem to have never left. They're said to be connected to the pennies that seem to show up from nowhere, and often owners and guests will catch a whiff of T.C.'s favorite cigar or Fannie's old-fashioned perfume.

Another spirit wandering the halls may be that of Mary Anne Wallace, a spinster sister of one of the 1870 owners. She's a short, stout, and quite buxom lady. She's seen wearing a blue-gray dress.

There's the ghost of a little white dog that likes to jump in bed with friendly guests. If he doesn't like the guests, he has no compunction against growling at them.

One ghost enjoys playing the harpsichord and the piano and may often wake guests with a serenade. Another ghost is a gadget freak. This spirit likes to fiddle with the household appliances, locking food in the digital oven while it's baking and fiddling with the computer keyboard.

The last two known spirits are that of Native Americans, who predate the mansion. They have been seen outside and have been heard playing their drums.

THE OLD EXCHANGE BUILDING AND PROVOST DUNGEON • CHARLESTON

Charleston, originally named Charles Towne in honor of England's King Charles II, was established in 1670. The first South Carolina settlement, it enjoyed a strong seafaring trade and was blessed with religious tolerance, two factors that contributed to a phenomenal growth. By 1742, Charles Towne had developed into the fourth largest city and was one of the wealthiest towns in colonial America. This phenomenal growth in trade necessitated the construction of a building to accommodate the heavy import-export market and as a place to conduct both public and private business.

The Exchange and Custom House was that building. Designed to reflect the self-image of the town's elite, it was erected in 1771 as one of the most important buildings in Charles Towne— indeed in the whole of colonial America. As the last building built by the British government in the American colonies, it served as the office for the king's customs collector

The Old Exchange and Provost Dungeon is supposedly haunted by pirates and Revolutionary War Patriots.
Courtesy of Old Exchange Archives.

and was used as a space for public gatherings and lavish entertainment.

Despite all its beauty and elegance, there was a sinister side of the building, for its nether regions housed a dank and dark dungeon. Called the Provost Dungeon, it was located deep beneath the Exchange Building, where men and women prisoners, transported in irons, were crowded together in squalor.

Although the Exchange and Custom House was built and first controlled by the British, it played an important role in American history. In 1773, Charles Towne citizens met in the

The Haunting of South Carolina

building's Great Hall to protest the Tea Act. While the citizens of Boston dumped their tea into the harbor, in Charles Towne it was seized and stored in the Exchange Building and was later sold to fund the patriot cause.

In 1774, South Carolina's delegates to the Continental Congress, the group that drafted the Declaration of Independence, were elected in the Great Hall. Then, in 1776, South Carolina declared Independence on the steps of the Exchange Building and Custom House. Charles Towne was the birthplace of three signers of the Declaration of Independence, and after they penned their names to that venerable document, the three—Arthur Middleton, Edward Rutledge, and Thomas Heyward Jr.—found themselves charged with treason by the British and tossed for a while into the filthy Provost dungeon.

They weren't the only patriots to be jailed; in 1780, after a lengthy siege, the British marched into Charles Towne and took over. They jailed leading citizens in the dungeon, requiring that they sign an oath to the King to secure their release.

Isaac Hayne was a South Carolina patriot who took the oath of allegiance to avoid imprisonment. His entire family was ill with smallpox in Charles Towne, and being incarcerated was not an option for him at that time. He was assured by the British that he would not be required to take up arms against his country. The British, however, broke their promise and drafted him into the Royal army.

Since they had broken their promise, Hayne decided he'd break his. He rejoined the American Army and fought against the British, who unfortunately captured him. Charged with treason, he was thrown into the Provost Dungeon. Without a jury trial, he was convicted and hanged within forty-eight hours.

As Hayne was being paraded through Charles Towne on the way to the gallows, his sister reportedly called out to him, "Come back, Isaac! Come back!" To which her brother replied, "I will if I can."

Many believe that Isaac Hayne has kept his promise. It's his ghost, they say, that haunts the Provost Dungeon and the Old Exchange Building, which now operates as a museum. Ghost tours also are conducted here, and reportedly on several occasions, there have been strange occurrences—unexplained shadows on the walls, chains swinging or rattling, strange noises—that were so frightening, the entire tour group broke and ran from the dungeon.

In addition to the ghost of Isaac Hayne, many believe the ghosts of Charleston's many pirates haunt the Old Exchange Building. In the late 1700s, Charles Towne was a favorite port for some of the Atlantic's most notorious pirates. The infamous Blackbeard, as a matter of fact, held the entire city for ransom, capturing vessels sailing into the harbor and taking hostages at will. He refused to release the hostages unless the town gave him much needed medical supplies.

Although many think the Old Exchange Building could be haunted by Blackbeard, others believe it's the ghost of another famous pirate. Stede Bonnet, known as the "Gentleman Pirate," was captured, along with his crew, in December 1718. Bonnet and twenty-two of his crew were hanged on December 10, 1718, at White Point. It seems likely that it's these old

The Haunting of South Carolina

buccaneers who are responsible for much of the building's poltergeist activity, which includes unexplained images and the balls of light known as "orbs" seen in many photographs taken here. Orbs and other flashes of light often captured on film are thought to be ghostly presences that are either too shy or too weak to make an appearance.

South Carolina is a hotbed, we tell you! A hotbed of UFO activity. Long before Captain Kirk began his journey where "no man has gone before," strange flying objects had been sighted in the skies over the Palmetto State. Most times, these sightings were a fun way to wonder if there really is someone out there. Others, such as the 1952 confidential report by the Atomic Energy Commission (now the Nuclear Regulatory Commission) of a sighting of four disk-shaped UFOs over the Savannah River nuclear plant, make you wonder if we should be worried someone is out there.

Worried or not, if UFOs are a particular interest, you're in luck. South Carolina has its own chapter of MUFON (Mutual UFO Network), the national UFO research, investigation, and reporting organization. South Carolina MUFON recently conducted an extensive investigation on the February 22, 2004 UFO sighting in Gaffney, where a brush fire is reported to have been started by strange sparks coming from the object. To read the report and for information on joining the organization, visit www.scmufon.org.

Eat, Drink, and Be Merry!

Eating out in Strange But True South Carolina is more than a meal: it's an experience. There are restaurants and bars galore along the back roads trail—some historic, some haunted, some just plain fun.

ADDY'S DUTCH CAFÉ & RESTAURANT • GREENVILLE

Well, the first thing you need to know about this restaurant is how to pronounce it. Forget that Southern drawl of yours and remember this is a Dutch café. What? Don't spreken de Dutch? OK, then. We'll tell ya. It's pronounced "Oddy," which is appropriate, really, considering that, as America's first authentic Dutch café, it's a bit of an oddity.

Addy opened the restaurant because he was homesick for a little bit of Holland, where the old café was a place for meeting with old friends and making new ones over good food and drink. Kind of a home away from home.

Located on Coffee Street, the restaurant is as close to an authentic brown café as you'll find outside of Amsterdam. There's hearty Dutch-style food, award-winning wine, more than forty imported beers, and live music weekly. Oh! And there's lots of fun and laughter to go around.

Located at 17 East Coffee Street.

Eat, Drink, and Be Merry!

ART BAR • COLUMBIA

It may be simply named, but it's also aptly named. This truly is an Art Bar. Thanks to local artists, there's art everywhere. Around the Front Bar. Around the Blue Lady Lounge. Around the dance floor. Even around the stall in the men's room!

Funky and fun, the Art Bar is a roadhouse with an urban flair. For example, it is considered by many as a biker bar. But you won't find your typical biker guy here. Nope. Those

Art Bar has won the Best People-Watching Bar Award.
Courtesy of Art Bar.

aren't Harleys parked out front. These bikes have names like Ducati, Moto Guzzi, BMW, and Suzuki.

In its quest to be all things to everyone, the Art Bar offers music, dancing, drinking, karaoke, improvisational comedy, and, of course, all that crazy artwork. Among its accolades you'll find the Best People-Watching Bar award and Best Bathroom Wall Wisdom award. So, come on in. Dance. Drink. Party. And before you leave, share your bathroom wisdom. It'll be the best night you'll never forget.

Located at 1211 Park Street.

AUNT SUE'S COUNTRY CORNER • PICKENS

Eating and shopping. Two of our most favorite pastimes. And we can do both at Aunt Sue's Country Corner. The restaurant, located right near Table Rock Park, offers a wonderful view

Aunt Sue's offers an assortment of eating and shopping pleasures, including homemade fudge.
Courtesy of Aunt Sue's Country Corner.

of Mother Nature while you enjoy Aunt Sue's tasty Southern-style sandwiches, including cream cheese and olives—a childhood favorite my father used make—chunky chicken salad, and their world-famous Reuben.

The dinner menu includes fried lobster tails, grilled salmon, steaks, shrimp and grits (another uniquely Southern dish), and liver and onions. There are fresh cobblers and ice cream for dessert, and you'll never make it out of the restaurant without a stop at the candy counter, where you'll find homemade fudge in such unusual flavors as pineapple upside down and peanut butter and jelly. And don't forget to stop at the specialty shops before you go.

Located at 107-A Country Creek Drive.

Eat, Drink, and Be Merry!

A.W. Shucks • Charleston

Aww, shucks. We just love the name of this long-time Charleston eatery. Opened in 1978, it quickly became a favorite, a place where locals came for fried shrimp,oysters on the half shell , and beer. The restaurant was, and still is, located within the Market area, an historic hub of activity in Charleston. For many years this was where Charlestonians shopped for produce, meats, and seafood.

The building housing the restaurant has an even longer history. Built by the National Biscuit Company—you many know them as Nabisco—more than seventy-five years ago, it became a "blind tiger" during prohibition. OK. We didn't know what that was either—we're not that old! Apparently "blind tiger" was the code word

A.W. Shucks is famous for its seafood.
Courtesy of CFC of Charleston Marketing Department.

for a place where illegal liquor was sold. Patrons paid a fee to "see a blind tiger." While waiting for this blind tiger to appear, they would be served drinks. After a few of those, we suppose, no one cared that the blind tiger never made an appearance.

In 1938, a tornado ripped through the Market area, taking the roof of the Blind Tiger, and maybe even that old blind tiger, with it. It lay fallow for many years, until someone came up with the idea to renovate and reinvigorate the area. A.W. Shucks opened and the rest is history.

Today, A.W. Shucks is a bit more upscale than just a place to get oysters and beer, although there's plenty to be had here. The menu now includes award-winning house specialties such as its stuffed shrimp, the secret-recipe seafood casserole, and the she-crab soup, which they claim as the Lowcountry's best. Guess the restaurant's motto says it all: "When you're in the mood for real seafood...come get fresh with us."

Located at 70 State Street.

BANTAM CHEF'S • CHESNEE

The fifties feel of Bantam Chef's appeals to young and old(er) alike. There are nifty retro booths, black-and-white tile floors, and cool decorations, such as model cars, license plates, and even a couple of full-sized Harleys.

You won't be able to miss the place either. It's the one with the banty rooster sign and the front end of a Studebaker mounted outside. It used to be a garage, by the way.

Located at Highway 11 and Highway 221 South.

BEACON DRIVE-IN • SPARTANBURG

Things are fast and furious at the Beacon Drive-In, the nation's second largest drive-in restaurant. Step in the door and you are ordered to "Call it out!" If you know what you want, you do, grab a tray, and head down the line. By the time you're reaching out for that big ol' glass of sweet tea, your order's up and you hurry off to find a seat. On a busy day, the Beacon will

The Beacon Drive-In opened in 1946.
Courtesy of Beacon Drive-In.

serve around five thousand people.

A regional landmark, with its distinctive red and white lighthouse sign, the Beacon Drive-In was opened in 1946 by John B. White Sr. He and his sons ran the restaurant for fifty years before turning it over to another local family, who has continued the restaurant's tradition of good food fast and lots of it.

The restaurant is open six days a week for breakfast, lunch, and dinner. In one week they prepare three tons of onions, three tons of potatoes, and four tons of beef, chicken, and seafood. The Beacon is the country's largest seller of sweet tea—and with good reason. They make it right—so sweet it makes your teeth hurt and served over shaved ice, with a lemon slice. They make 62,500 gallons of tea a week, sweetened with three thousand pounds of sugar.

The Beacon Drive-In is a South Carolina tradition you don't want to miss!

Located at 255 John B. White Sr. Boulevard.

BLACKSTONE'S CAFÉ • BEAUFORT

Blackstone's Café is a quaint little breakfast and lunch place. Tucked away on a side street, it's filled from top to bottom with all manner of marine and nautical gee gaws and memorabilia. It's a veritable museum. But that's not what brings folks in from miles around. Naw. It's the food that draws them in.

Blackstone's serves homemade specialties for both breakfast and lunch. There are shrimp and grits—a big bowl full, filled with fluffy grits, a myriad of shrimp, and topped with melted cheese. The omelets aren't your every day break-a-few-eggs-and-call-it-a-day either. It's never too early for seafood, so try the Shrimp Omelet, filled inside and out with shrimp, demi-glaze, and cheese.

Oh! And Blackstone's is wired! So bring your laptop, grab a table and a cuppa joe, and hang out for a while!

Located at 205 Scotts Street.

BOOKSTORE CAFÉ • CHARLESTON

Now here's a restaurant after my own heart. Housed in a circa 1890 bookstore, it has a rustic ambience and the warmth of a family-owned café—which, of course, it is. And, boy, can these folks cook Southern. Southern with an imaginative twist, that is.

You can get breakfast all day or choose from the lunch menu, where the Island Potato Casseroles, topped with eggs and a

Eat, Drink, and Be Merry!

giant, fluffy sweet potato biscuit, are the signature dishes. And you java lovers won't want to miss out on the Bookstore's specially blended coffee. Almost strong enough to stand a spoon in, it's been featured in the book, *Coffee Experience of Charleston*.

With its exposed brick walls and whimsical "book" wallpaper, the Bookstore Café is a favorite of the locals, who come to meet with friends and tuck into the mega-sized meals. Although it's been named "One of the Best Neighborhood Restaurants in the South" by *Bon Appétit* magazine, the owners haven't let it go to their heads. The meals are reasonably priced and, as we said, mega-sized.

Located at 412 King Street.

Chapin Station Restaurant • Chapin

Chapin may be a small town, but it's chock full of restaurants. As the quintessential ribs and burgers joint, Chapin Station is one of the hot spots. Their motto is, "Hard core food & laid back fun."

Chapin Station's menu is extensive. In addition to their ribs—available in every fever, from mild to suicide—they feature burgers, sandwiches, pastas, ribs, steaks, and chicken. The seafood menu is quite interesting. Besides snow crab legs and steamed oysters, you can find some unusual dishes, such as the Beaufort Stew, a mixture of shrimp, sausage, potatoes, onions, and corn, seasoned with bay and steamed. If you're really hungry for seafood, you can try the Ultimate Steam Pot, which is filled with steamed oysters, mussels, shrimp, crab legs, crawfish, corn on the cob, and potatoes.

Located at 1260 Chapin Road.

CHARLIE'S STEAK HOUSE • GREENVILLE

Charlie's is an institution in Greenville. Billed as South Carolina's oldest family-owned steak house, it opened in 1921, when Texan Charlie Efstration saw a need. Charlie was fresh out of the service, when a visit to his brother brought him to Greenville. A former restaurant owner, he found the town lacking a restaurant that served steaks like he'd enjoyed in the West—thick, juicy, and full of flavor.

Greenville residents apparently agreed, for the business grew. In 1933, Charlie purchased an old produce market at the restaurant's present location and renovated it. It was located directly across the street from the local YMCA and during the hard times of the depression, Charlie provided soup and bread to those in the food lines and to the schools so that the children would have a hot meal.

It wasn't all hard times, though. In 1935, a local radio station began broadcasting a nightly program from the restaurant. Featuring live bands, the program drew in huge crowds, giving birth to the dinner and dancing concept in Greenville.

After their tour of duty in World War II, Charlie's sons, Peter and Paul, joined the business, where they remain today. Paul, in fact, hand-cuts the on-premises dry aged beef.

Yes, you can get other things at Charlie's—seafood, chicken, even pork. But Charlie's is a steak house and steak is what they do. They serve only the highest quality cuts, and they're not stingy with them. The Extra Large Thick Sirloin is often mistaken for a roast! No spices or tenderizers

Eat, Drink, and Be Merry!

are added, so you get only the wonderfully tender flavor of the beef.

Located at 18 East Coffee Street.

CHEESEBURGER IN PARADISE • GREENVILLE/MYRTLE BEACH

We know this is one of those cheesy chain restaurants, but we're big ol' Parrotheads and we just can't resist a taste of the islands. The star of Cheeseburger in Paradise's menu is, of course, the Cheeseburger in Paradise—lettuce, tomato, Heinz 57, onion slice, and a big ol' kosher pickle. Comes with French fried potatoes, but you have to order the cold draught beer. And of course you can get your cheeseburger any way you want it—even if you want to leave off the big hunk of meat. See, you can substitute a veggie burger in any of the burgers.

They also serve stuff like BBQ Jerk Ribs, St. Barts Blackened Chicken, Nawlins BBQ Shrimp, and Shrimp Po' Boy Wrap. Wash it all down with a frozen Buffett-themed concoction, such as the Electric Lizard or the Montserrat Volcano and save room for Some Kind of Sensuous Treat—the wacky chocolate nachos or ummm...Key Lime Pie.

Housed in a weathered beach house, this paradise is the quickest way to escape the daily rat race and sail away to Margaritaville. So drag out the blown-out flops, throw on some baggy shorts, and bone up on the Buffett lyrics. Time to go searchin' for that lost shaker of salt.

Located at 535B Haywood Road, Greenville, and 7211 North Kings Highway, Myrtle Beach.

CIRCA 1886 • CHARLESTON

The Wentworth Mansion is one of Charleston's premier luxury inns. Indeed, it's one of the finest in the world. Built in 1886, it was the private home of wealthy Charlestonian,

Circa 1886 is located on the grounds of Wentworth Mansion.
Courtesy of Circa 1886.

Silas Rodgers, who obviously had a taste for the finer things in life. The inn, unchanged since its construction, is richly appointed with marble fireplaces, intricate woodwork, and Tiffany stained-glass windows.

Located on the grounds of Wentworth Mansion, you'll find Circa 1886, a fine dining restaurant. And, we do mean fine dining. This is five-star dining at its best. The menu reads like a symphony. Five-course dinners offer elegant dishes such as Brandy Carrot Soup, Pecan Pickled Palm Heart, Key Lime and Coconut Crusted Salmon, and Fried Heirloom Okra.

A nice accompaniment to your symphonic meal is a choice from Circa's extensive wine list. The list, which changes daily, boasts 280 selections from all over the world. As a grand finale, try something from the Patisserie, such as the Strawberry

Eat, Drink, and Be Merry!

Shortcake Souffle or the Charleston Sweet Summers–peach cobbler topped with blackberry sherbet and accompanied by a Raspberry Lemonade Smoothie.

Circa 1886 has been raved about in such prestigious foodie publications as *Bon Appétit*, *Wine Spectator* Magazine, *Food and Wine* Magazine, and *Conde Nast Traveler*. It's a Charleston symphony you don't want to miss. So pull out your Sunday best and come on down.

Located at 149 Wentworth Street.

Crabby Mike's Seafood Company • Surfside Beach

Feelin' a bit crabby? Well, join Crabby Mike, the crabbiest ol' salt around, for his all-you-can-eat seafood buffet. With 180 items on the buffet—including, of course, crab legs—there's no way you're leaving here hungry. You'll find seafood any way you want it, fried, steamed, broiled, baked, and boiled.

Crabby Mike's been servin' up the seafood on Surfside Beach for seventeen

Crabby Mike's has a 180-item buffet.
Courtesy of Crabby Mike's Seafood Company.

years. Despite the roominess of the restaurant, nicknamed Crabbersville, there's usually a bit of wait, but wait. You'll be glad you did. Check out all that nautical and marine décor while you're sitting there—boats and schools of colorful fishes hanging from the ceiling, stuffed fishes on the walls, and a huge underwater-scene mural. The kids are gonna love it.

Located at 290 Highway 17 North.

DRUNKEN JACK'S • MURRELLS INLET

You knew there'd be a story behind the name of this restaurant, didn't ja? Seems that back in the days of yore, that most famous of blackguards, Edward Teach, aka Blackbeard the Pirate, plied the waters up and down the South Carolina coast. Following a particularly big hijacking of rum, Blackbeard and his men put in at Murrells Inlet. After burying most of the rum, they partied hardy, enjoying the island's bounty of shrimp, oysters, and fresh-caught fish washed down with their purloined rum.

They next day dawned bright and despite their monumental hangovers, all pirates once again boarded the *Queen Anne's Revenge*, Blackbeard's ship, and set sail for the blue waters of the Caribbean. All pirates, that is, save one. Old Jack was so hung over, it seems, that he missed the boat and was left stranded on the deserted island. Just him and all that rum.

Well, it was two years before the *Queen Anne's Revenge* made it back to Murrells Inlet. Blackbeard and his men disembarked and set out to dig up the rum, oh, and maybe they'd pick up ol' Jack if he was still around. Well, guess what, folks? What they found was a bunch of empty rum kegs strewn up and down the beach and, bleaching in the sun beneath a palmetto tree, they found ol' Jack's bones. So, that's how the island came to be known as Drunken Jack's Island, and that's how the restaurant got its name.

No doubt you've figured out that Drunken Jack's is a seafood restaurant. Yes, they serve beef. And, yes, they serve chicken. But seafood is the specialty. Hungry? Try Drunken Jack's Shore Dinner. It's a seafood feast, beginning with she crab soup followed by a platter of flounder, shrimp, oysters, devil crab, and lobster. Maybe wash it down with a little rum. You have to pay for it though.

Located at 4031 Highway 17 Business.

FLO'S PLACE • MURRELLS INLET

The first thing you'll notice about Flo's Place is all the hats. There are hats on the walls and hats on the ceilings—round about three thousand of 'em, just hanging there. The whole hat thing started way back in the day, when proprietor Flo began stealing them from her patrons and hanging them up. Guess money was too tight for a decorating budget. Anyhoo, the idea caught on and now folks bring hats from all over the world and leave 'em hanging in Flo's.

The second thing you notice about Flo's place is that everybody seems to be having fun. Maybe it's the Dixieland music permeating the place. Or the Mardi Gras theme. Or maybe it's just all that good, cold beer. Whatever the reason, when folks step through the door, they leave their cares behind and "Laissez Les Bon Temp Rouler!"

Even the food at Flo's Place is fun. Ragin' Cajun is the style here. Start out with a big ol' bowl of Alligator Stew or some Alligator Nuggets. Better yet, try some a Dem Gator Bones. Yes, it's really alligator leg sections, marinated and served with Flo's own honey mustard barbecue sauce.

Flo's main feast specialty is the Dunkin' Pot for two, a huge pot filled with oysters, clams, shrimp, potatoes, and seasonal shellfish such as mussels, crawfish, or crab claws, and topped with your choice of either Snow Crab legs or one whole Maine lobster. It's served with garlic bread and a rich dunkin' sauce.

Next time you're in Murrell's Inlet, don't miss the chance to stop in at Flo's Place. Hang your hat, stay for a while, and as the Cajuns say, "pass a good time."

Located at 3797 Highway 17 Business.

THE FLYING SAUCER • COLUMBIA

If you're a beer lover and/or a party animal you're gonna want Scottie to beam you over here. There are around eighty brews on tap and up to 150 different bottled beers. They've got something going on pretty much every night of the week, with live music on the weekends. You might want to try Wednesday, which is Brewery Nite. You get a special deal, where you buy the beer and can then buy the glass for cost. Start your own collection!

Located at 931 Senate Street.

Eat, Drink, and Be Merry!

THE FROSTY FROG CAFÉ • HILTON HEAD

According to legend, Frosty was a frog that took the scenic route to Hilton Head. Seems he spent his tadpole years in Eerie, Pennsylvania, but the chilly winters were just too much for the cold-natured little amphibian. So he packed his bags and moved south, settling first in Charlotte, North Carolina, where he opened a bar and became well-known for blending up some frosty concoctions.

Ah, but Frosty was still not happy, or so the legend goes. He needed sand and sea. So, once again he packed it in and headed south. This time, it seems, he's finally found home.

On Hilton Head, Frosty's opened a little café, where he's once again becoming well-known for his frosty concoctions. You can find all kinds of weird daiquiri flavors here. Try the Banana Banshee or maybe the Jungle Juice, reputed to be a tropical delight to make the natives dance! There're Rum Runners, Hurricanes, Blue Hawaiis, and Pina Coladas.

If you'd like to take the party with you, you can get any of Frosty's frosties to go—by the gallons. They even advertise it by the truck load—with a twenty-four hour notice. Call for a quote. There's food to go with those daiquiris, and it's probably a good idea to eat a little something to help absorb all that alcohol.

Located at 1 Forest Beach in Colingy Plaza.

GULLAH CUISINE • MT. PLEASANT

West African slaves were brought to South Carolina in 1670 to work the rice, indigo, and cotton plantations. With them came their superior knowledge of rice cultivation and, like a secret treasure, the remembrance of a rich heritage. Through the centuries, this heritage—the heritage of the Gullah people—developed into a unique culture.

Blending African traditions with Lowcountry customs, it permeates the South, nowhere more than in its cuisine. Though it's often known as "soul food," it's the food we grew up on. Shrimp and grits, gumbo, oyster dressing, these Lowcountry favorites all have their roots in African tradition.

At Gullah Cuisine, owner Charlotte Jenkins remains true to the Gullah culture. Her peppery Gullah Rice, a rich mahogany color, is filled with shrimp, chicken, sausage, and vegetables. It makes a wonderful meal on its own and can be served as a side with any of the main dishes. The lunch buffet features all your favorites—collards, okra soup, green beans, succotash, and cabbage. You'll also find gumbo, barbecue pork and chicken, and fried and baked chicken. They serve a more formal menu at dinner.

The restaurant is decorated with arts and crafts that feature the Gullah heritage. There is a selection of handmade sweet grass baskets for sale, along with Gullah seasonings so you can bring the taste home with you.

Located at 1717 Highway 17 North.

THE HANDLEBAR • GREENVILLE

Good food. Good music. Lots of beer. What more can you ask for? The Handlebar: A Listening Room is one of upstate South Carolina's premier concert venues. Already popular as a music hall, the Handlebar moved into new digs in 2001 and put a new focus on its food menu. Man-sized sandwiches, wraps, soups, salads, onion rings, and fries dominate the menu—topped by one of Greenville's best deserts, a huge slice of Kahlua cake. Come eat early and get primed for a night of good music.

It's with good reason that the Handlebar is considered a top venue in South Carolina, indeed in the Southeast. The concert hall features a wide variety of music genres, from Rock to Reggae and everything in between. Artists who've performed here include: Joan Baez, John Mayer, Ricky Skaggs, Nappy Roots, Leon Redbone, Doc Watson, Little Feat, and The Amazing Rhythm Aces, just to name a few.

Located at 304 East Stone Avenue.

HOMINY GRILL • CHARLESTON

The building that houses this Southern comfort food restaurant is at least as interesting as the food and that's pretty darned interestin'. Built in 1897, the three-story shotgun dwelling reflects the architectural style of a nineteenth century home. The ground floor, where the restaurant is housed, was once a barbershop and still contains the original hardwood floors and pounded tin ceiling.

Now for the food...It's another case of Southern food with flair. Breakfast and brunch are hearty favorites—eggs and country ham with high-rise biscuits and, of course, hominy grits. The omelets are imaginative, such as the Lowcountry made with red rice and shrimp gravy. Another interesting dish is the shrimp sautéed with scallions, mushrooms, and bacon over cheese grits.

For lunch you might want to sample the BLT. It's made with fried green tomatoes! Dinners are imaginative. For a small plate, you might want to try the sautéed chicken livers with shiitake mushrooms and sweet red peppers served over angel hair pasta. Or maybe you'd like to try the vegetable plate. It's just a tad different than the one grandma would make: Lima beans, baked cheese grits,

Hominy Grill serves Southern food with flair.
Photo by Peter Frank Edwards.
Courtesy of Hominy Grill.

sautéed greens, okra beignets, and cornbread. Even the fried chicken's different—it comes with spiced peach sauce. Like we said, Southern with flair.

Located at 207 Rutledge Avenue.

HOT FISH CLUB • MURRELLS INLET

This restaurant is rooted in Murrells Inlet history, which became something of a summer resort for wealthy families in the 1800s. The original Hot and Hot Fish Club was established as a social club where the good ol' boys came to dine on extravagant meals, drink fine wine, and enjoy a little male bonding.

That was then and this is now. Today's Hot Fish Club, located near the original site of the historic club, is a place for everyone to enjoy extravagant meals, fine wine, and entertainment. Fine dinners and wine are offered in the restaurant, after which you may want to sashay out to the Gazebo, billed as the hottest place on the inlet for live entertainment.

Located at 4911 Highway 17 Business.

HUDSON'S ON THE DOCKS • HILTON HEAD

This restaurant claims to be world famous, and with Hilton Head being an international tourist spot, it may well be. We know it's got a lot of tradition here on the little island that started out as a good place to hunt and fish and cut timber.

That tradition started back in the roaring twenties, when J.B. Hudson Sr. bought the oyster factory that had been built

At Hudson's on the Docks, diners can watch shrimp boats unload their catch.
Courtesy of Hudson's on the Docks.

on the docks in 1912. The family-run business resulted in the Oyster Factory Dining Room, where the Hudsons served up their freshly harvested oysters. It wasn't until 1995 that J.B. Hudson Jr., who had taken over the business from his dad, added shrimping to the operation. Two years and a lot of shrimp in the nets later, he opened Hudson's Seafood Restaurant.

Today, Hudson's, now owned by the Carmine family, employs the largest of only two fleets left on the island. One of the biggest attractions of eating here is to watch the fleet come in, bringing their load of shrimp, oysters, and other seafood to the docks.

Located at 1 Hudson Road.

Under the impression that Hilton Head Island is named for that hotel family? Well, you're wrong. Hilton Head was named for Captain William Hilton, the English explorer, who "discovered" the place in 1663 while checking out real estate for some Barbados planters. In typical explorer fashion, ol' Bill stuck his own name on the place.

JAMMIN' JAVA • COLUMBIA

There's a good reason this place is named Jammin' Java: the joint jams with live music, and although it caters to the younger crowd—mostly college students and young career folks—we old folks can hang, too. That is, if our walkers will make it down that steep flight of stairs that lead to this subterranean café.

Eat, Drink, and Be Merry!

Jammin' Java is open for breakfast, lunch, and dinner. They offer muffins, croissants, and fruit for breakfast, and you'll find an extensive menu of deli sandwiches, pizza, and salads for lunch and dinner. Sorry, folks, no alcohol is served, which is a bummer if you like a little brew with your music. But, hey, try a couple of quad shot mochas. They're guaranteed to give ya a buzz!

Located at 1530 Main Street Suite D.

The Jazz Corner • Hilton Head

This place is jazzy! Opened by well-known jazz musician Bob Masteller and business partner, Charles Swift, the Jazz Corner is an elegant establishment that puts equal emphasis on music and menu.

Local, national, and international jazz musicians are showcased in this uniquely designed club, which has won awards for its acoustics. The food is American eclectic gourmet at reasonable prices. And if you just gotta dance, don't worry, there are two dance floors where you can trip the light fantastic.

Located at 1000 William Hilton Parkway Suite C1.

JB's Smokeshack • Goose Creek/John's Island

There's nothing more hotly debated in the South than just what's the best way to burn a pig. Or just what you should put on it—if anything—once it's burned. At JB's Smokeshack they slow cook their pigs over hickory, a method that allows the meat to cook without drying out and that imbues it with a densely smoky flavor. (The chicken is smoked over apple wood.) Once it's done, it's pulled from the bone and lightly chopped. As for what to put on it? Well, their motto is "The Flavor's in the Meat, The Sauce is on the Side." So, nothing is a good choice. If you gotta have sauce, they offer three: Vinegar-based, similar to the type that

JB's Smokeshack is one of the many places in South Carolina that is famous for its barbecue.
Courtesy of JB's Smokeshack.

originated in Lexington, North Carolina; spicy, reminiscent of a Memphis-style tomato-based sauce; and South Carolina-style mustard-based.

You can get all the usual sides and maybe a couple of more—potato salad, barbecued beans, potato salad, cole slaw, okra gumbo, black-eyed peas, and collards—all made with fresh Lowcountry veggies, when in season.

Located at 521 Redbank Road in Goose Creek, and 3406 Maybank Highway in John's Island.

POOGAN'S PORCH • CHARLESTON

Oooo! We just love a restaurant with a story! This one's got two. First is the story behind the restaurant's unusual name. Seems more than twenty-five years ago, this 1886 Victorian

Eat, Drink, and Be Merry!

building was the last non-commercial holdout on Queen Street. The family finally gave in and sold the home to someone wanting to turn it into a restaurant.

Poogan's Porch is supposedly haunted by Zoe St. Armand.
Courtesy of Poogan's Porch.

When the family moved out, a neighborhood dog stayed on. He'd claimed the porch as his, and stayed there through the construction and renovation. When the restaurant opened, he became the official greeter, welcoming folks onto his porch with a wag of the tail. He went to that great porch in the sky in 1979 and is buried in the front garden, but his spirit lives on in the name of this fine restaurant.

The second story is a delicious ghost story. Seems that around the turn of the century, the home was owned by two little spinster sisters. By all accounts, Elizabeth and Zoe St. Armand lived a solitary and lonely existence, just the two of them rambling around in that big old house. When Elizabeth died in 1945, Zoe became quite depressed. She died several years later.

It's Zoe's lonely spirit that is thought to be haunting Poogan's Porch. Folks have reported seeing a woman in a severe black dress inside the restaurant at night. Throughout the years, many calls have gone out to the police about a woman locked in the restaurant. She's banging on the door, they say, wanting out. Of course, when the police arrive, there's no one there. Zoe also has been known to knock on the bathroom door when it's occupied and has scared the wits outta guests by appearing behind them in the bathroom mirror.

What's even better is that in addition to its stories, Poogan's Porch serves up some mighty fine food. Since its opening in 1976, it's become a Charleston hotspot and a place where visiting celebrities come to nosh and enjoy the Lowcountry ambiance. Barbra Streisand has eaten here. So has Paul Newman. Martha Stewart raves about the place. You will too.

Located at 72 Queen Street.

> South Carolina's distinctive mustard-based barbecue sauce is the product of the state's large German heritage, which came here in the 1700s. After almost three hundred years, the German community is still prominent in South Carolina's barbecue industry. The Bessinger family is the largest seller of the mustard-based sauces and family names such as Shealy, Hite, Sweatman, Price, and Ziegler offer some of the state's best 'cue.

REDBONE ALLEY • FLORENCE/SUMTER

Regardless of the name, this restaurant's no dog. First opened in Florence, the restaurant is housed in the old J.C. Penny's building, on which owner Dale Barth did a remarkable renovation. Stripping off the roof, he had another floor added. With the massive height and open space, he recreated the feel of an outdoor Charleston café.

A steel two-story façade was then constructed, which flanks and overlooks the streetscape. It's a dramatic scene—a two-story-high space with an open atrium, a back porch with lanterns aglow, and even a patio for the kiddies, with an old Good Humor ice cream truck to explore. There's a balcony overlook and a sports bar and grill. Murals by noted Charleston artist David Boatwright festoon the place with Lowcountry landscapes. The second location in Sumter was built from scratch, using the original as a blueprint.

As for the food, Barth calls his cuisine New Southern Fusion. Whatever. Critics and just plain folks agree: It's tail-waggin' good.

Located at 1903 West Palmetto Street, Florence, and1342 Broad Street, Sumter.

STICKY FINGERS • MT. PLEASANT AND BEYOND

So what do you get when you eat really good barbecue? What else? Sticky fingers! That wasn't the main inspiration for the name of the highly successful barbecue joint that started out in little Mount Pleasant. Owners Todd Eischeid, Jeff Goldstein, and Chad Walldorf, friends since junior high, say the name was inspired by that seventies Rolling Stones album cover by Andy Warhol. Those of you of a certain age know the one. We're not really sure why it was the inspiration, but, hey, it does make a great name for a ribs joint.

Anyhoo, the three native Chattanoogans opened that first restaurant in 1992 and things just took off from there. They now have locations all over the Southeast. There's good reason for that. They do good 'cue. It's the slow cookin' what does it, they say. The ribs are the most popular item. They come in five styles—Memphis-style wet, Memphis-style dry, Tennessee Whiskey, Habanero Hot, and Carolina Sweet. However you order 'em, though, plan on making a mess. You have to. It's the law. Can't eat ribs without getting sticky fingers—and face. No problem here. Your silverware comes wrapped in a hand towel instead of a napkin.

Located all over.

Remember ol' Snap, Crackle, and Pop, those three little Rice Krispies elves? Well, those fey little creatures were created in Rock Hill, South Carolina. Seems cartoon illustrator Vernon Grant of Rock Hill got the idea in 1933 from a Rice Krispies radio ad: "Listen to the fairy song of health, the merry chorus sung by Kellogg's Rice Krispies as they snap, crackle, and pop in a bowl of milk. If you've never heard food talking, now's your chance." Oh, yeah. That's inspiring. Anyway, Grant came up with the characters and presented them to Kellogg's, who loved 'em right away. The rest is advertising history.

Here are some of South Carolina's Strange But True town names:

Clio
Ah, how poetic! This little town was named for one of the nine goddesses in Greek mythology known as muses. Clio is the muse of history and historical/heroic poetry.

Irmo
The name is derived from two of the town's prominent citizens: C.J. Iredell and H.C. Moseley, both railroad men.

Ninety-Six
The name of this town came from traders in the 1700s, who mistakenly thought ninety-six was the number of miles from this location to the Cherokee village of Keowee.

Pumpkintown
Pumpkintown was established in 1745, when the first settler, Cornelius Keith, traded a pony to an Indian chief for a small tract of land he could call his own. The soil was rich, and the place grew some mighty big pumpkins. It soon became a bustling settlement and one night, folks got together to come up with a name for the place. They couldn't agree on a name until one drunk Irish man stood up and slurred, "Jest quit arguin' and call it Punkin Town."

Funny Happenings Here

Pig pickin' and oyster shuckin'. Chitlin's on parade and okras astrut. There's just no end to the funny goings on in Strange But True South Carolina.

A(GUSTA) BAKER'S DOZEN • COLUMBIA

Yeah, yeah, we were confused, too. But it's really quite simple. This storytelling festival is held to honor the works of nationally-known author and storyteller Augusta Baker, who had the good sense to move to Columbia in 1980.

Born in 1911, Baker was introduced to literature by her schoolteacher parents. She taught school for several years, but in 1937, she was appointed as children's librarian at the 135th Street branch of the New York Public Library in Harlem. Here, she helped to start a search for children's literature that portrayed African-Americans as something more than servile buffoons that spoke in crude dialect, an effort that lead to the first collection of bibliographies of books for and about African-American children.

In 1953, Augusta was appointed storytelling specialist and assistant coordinator of children's services. In 1961, she became the coordinator of children's services, the first African-American to hold an administrative position in the New York Public Library system. During this time, she continued her search for appropriate children's literature for African-Americans, both by authoring books herself and by encouraging publishers to search out good children's literature. Baker retired in 1980 and came to South Carolina, where she was appointed the Storyteller-In-Residence for the University of South Carolina—the first such position at any American university—a position she held until her death in 1998.

The A(gusta) Baker's Dozen strives to continue Baker's mission of opening the world of other cultures to children, crossing racial, social, and geographical boundaries. Sponsored by the Richland County Public Library and the School of Library and Information Science, the festival features local and national storytellers spinning their tales for children of all ages. The weekend kicks off with a special storytelling event for two thousand area children and concludes with a three-hour outdoor event for the entire family. This event features music, theater, and storytelling for all ages.

Held annually in April.

BLUE CRAB FESTIVAL • LITTLE RIVER

Little River's got crabs, and they're proud of 'em! In fact, for the past twenty-five years, they've been feting the colorful little crustacean with a big ol' party. Held on the historic waterfront, the festival features live music. Take your pick to beat your feet to. There's everything from jazz, to country, to beach, to gospel (now that's really rockin'!). There's a beauty pageant, a classic car show, a juried arts and crafts show, and lots of stuff for the kiddies, including an art contest and a fishing tournament. Wow! Oh, what? We forgot something?

Oh, yeah. Food. Blue crab is, after all, a premier seafood. And you'll find lots of little crabbies to nosh on, but there are lots more than that. There's plenty of other sea creatures available and if you're not so hot on seafood, you'll find hot dogs, hamburgers, pizza, and all types of deserts, just whatever your little tummy desires. Come join the fun. You'll be glad Little River's got crabs.

Held annually in May.

Little River celebrates its history with the Blue Crab Festival. Courtesy of Calabash Photography Studio, Little River Chamber of Commerce and Visitor's Center.

CAROLINA Q CUP • COLUMBIA

Did we mention that barbecue was a South Carolina staple? We thought so. Did we also mention that there's types of 'cue sauce? Well, in case we didn't, there are. There's heavy tomato-based, light tomato-based, vinegar and pepper, and mustard-based, which originated in this great state. South Carolinians love their 'cue. And, they're lucky. They're blessed to live in the only state in the union that cooks and serves all four types of 'cue sauce: There's just one problem. No one can figure out who makes the best 'cue. Ah ha! Let's have a cook off!

The Carolina Q Cup pits (get it? Pit? Barbecue...oh, never mind.) the state's best barbecuers against each other to see just who does the best 'cue, not only in the state, but in the world. See, the way they figure it, since the Palmetto state is the only state to cook with all four sauces, then the 'cue that wins the Carolina Q Cup can truly be proclaimed as the world's best. We say go for it!

The championship features two professional categories—wood or charcoal and gas or electric. Each professional team prepares a whole hog, with judging criteria based on taste, tenderness, appearance—not only of the meat but also of the personal appearance of the cooks and their cooking area. The judging is done by Certified South Carolina Barbecue Judges. Certified!

In addition to the professional categories, teams from the U.S. Army, the South Carolina Highway Patrol, the Columbia Fire Department, and other service and military organizations are invited. Prizes are awarded to the teams deemed best by the CERTIFIED judges. The Grand Champion receives the coveted silver Carolina Q Cup. And bragging rights.

Held annually in October.

CHITLIN' STRUT • SALLEY

Now, if you're a true Southerner, born and raised, you at least know what chitlin's are. You may not've had the "guts" to eat them, but you've heard of 'em. You newcomer Southerners may actually have heard of them, too; you just may not recognize 'em by their proper pronunciation. See, chitlin' is the Southern way to say chitterling. You know, pig guts, uh, intestines.

Chitlin's, boiled to tenderness then battered and fried, have long been a Southern…delicacy?…that helped keep folks going in lean times. And, ironically, that's what chitlin's have done in Salley. They've helped the town keep going in lean times.

The whole thing got started back in 1966, when then-mayor Jack Able found the town was in dire need of new Christmas decorations. Ahh, but times were lean for the little town of maybe four hundred. Where were they going to come up with the money? Able took his dilemma to local DJ, "Friendly" Ben Dekle, who suggested, of all things, a Chitlin' Strut. The city council agreed, and on the day after Thanksgiving, the very first Chitlin' Strut was held.

Today Salley's Chitlin' Strut is internationally famous. Every year, more than fifty thousand folks flock into this little burg to laugh and dance and eat…or not…a little pig guts. OK, a lot of them are at least sampling, because in 2004, ten thousand pounds of chitlin's were consumed. Now that's a lot of…well, whatever. They're brave souls, too, for the smell of chitlin's cooking is enough to make you lose your lunch!

We'd like to tell you that chitlin's don't really strut in this famous festival, but the fact is, sometimes they do. In the parade. Seems that sometimes folks parade around in the parade with chitlin's hanging off 'em. We're only going to assume this is for show and those chitlin's aren't the ones being cooked up.

Funny Happenings Here

In addition to the parade, there's all manner of revelin' going on. There's the Chitlin' Strut dance contest and a Chitlin' Strut Beauty Pageant. How cool would it be to be crowned Miss Chitlin' Strut?

Of course, there's lots and lots of food. And not just chitlin's. But, then again, you came all this way! Be brave! Just hold your nose and take a bite!

Held annually over the Thanksgiving holiday weekend.

COLLARD FESTIVAL • GASTON

We Southerners sure like to celebrate our food, don't we? At least this one's a healthy one. OK, so we take out a little of that healthiness when we cook 'em up with fat back or bacon grease, but there's nothin' better than a big ol' mess of greens! Add some fried pork chops, black-eyed peas, and mashed taters, and we're in heaven.

Anyhoo...Gaston celebrates collards every year with a big ol' festival. There's a parade, a talent contest, a beauty pageant, karaoke, an auction, arts and crafts, carnival rides, live entertainment, and collards. The ladies of Gaston cook 'em up, using their own secret recipe. And if you don't like collards (banish the thought!) there's still plenty of other food to eat.

Held annually in September.

COME-SEE-ME • ROCK HILL

Jumpin' Jehosaphats! The folks of Rock Hill are so proud of their pretty town that they're throwin' a party and they want you to come. The Come-See-Me Festival is South Carolina's largest all-volunteer festival. Attracting more than 125,000 every year, it's ranked in the Southeast's Top 20 Spring Festivals.

The festival was the brainchild of then-mayor, later State Senator C.H. "Icky" Albright, who was encouraged by Rock Hill citizen, Vernon Grant, creator of those whimsical Rice Krispies fairies Snap, Crackle, and Pop. Grant created Glen the Frog to serve as the festival mascot. Starting out as a weekend event to showcase the town and its Glencairn Garden in full bloom, it was such a success that today it runs for a full ten days.

And, boy, are those jam-packed with fun things to see and do. There are pancake breakfasts, a Come-See-Me Parade, a tennis tournament, a golf tournament, a gourmet grill off, a one-act play festival, living history events, softball games, a tailgate party, a charity ball, live entertainment in Glencairn Garden, a Canine Disc Competition, a family carnival, Shakespearean plays, art exhibitions, a beach bash, a funny run (where folks dress up in funny clothes), and concerts. Whew!

The kids figure big in this festival. They'll have hoppin' good fun with such events as the Mayor's Frog Jump, where they can bring their own frogs to compete or borrow one. There's also a Special Olympics competition, an indoor youth climbing competition, a Teddy Bear Tea Party, a build-your-own sundae with Glen the Frog event, and Jumping Jeepers Frog Crafts. In the Glencairn Garden event, parents and kids get to make their own fun by acting out nursery rhymes with Mother Goose, making goose puppets, frog crafts, face painting, and sidewalk chalk drawings. The festival concludes with a big Fireworks Extravaganza.

Held annually in April.

Funny Happenings Here

FLOPEYE FISH FESTIVAL • GREAT FALLS

Those folks in Great Falls, also known as Flopeye, are our kind of folks. How could they not be with a motto that proclaims "After all, life is to enjoy." Amen, brother.

These nice folks aren't above a little good-natured ribbing, either. According to town legend, more than seventy years ago one of the local merchants, a fellow named Andy Morrison, had a set of pretty prominent eyelids. Seems ol' Ang had a habit of sitting outside in front of his general store, where inevitably those big ol' eyelids of

The Flopeye Fish Festival has a children's area with rides.
Photo by Todd Wright.

his would start to droop, flopping, as it were, over his eyes. Well, one day a lady who'd never met Andy was strolling by. "Who is that old flop-eyed man?" she blurted out. Her question was overheard and it spread like wildfire through the community. It finally reached Rob Mebane, president of the Republic Cotton Mill, who commented that Flopeye was a good name for that part of town.

Now we're not sure, that might not have been a compliment, but the folks in that area of town know what life is all about. They know not to sweat the small stuff, and they keep in mind that it's all small stuff! So they adopted the name as their own and began announcing to anyone who asked that they were from Flopeye. Somehow through the years that name has stuck.

Every Memorial Day weekend, the folks of Flopeye throw a party that serves as a reunion and a way to celebrate their community. There are all kinds of food, live entertainment, car shows, arts and crafts, carnival rides, and games. It's a celebration of life guaranteed to keep your eyelids from flopping!

Held annually on Memorial Day weekend.

FLYING PIG KITE FESTIVAL • PORT ROYAL

Did you know that pigs fly in Port Royal? Well, it only happens on the Fourth of July, but it's truly a high-flying event! At the Flying Pig Kite Festival, professional kite flyers (hey, how do you get that job?) take to the beach and fill the skies with their kites of many colors—and sizes, from two feet to eighty feet.

Now, if you're wondering why the good folks of Port Royal chose a flying pig as its festival symbol, well, just think of it, what animal attends more outdoor events in South Carolina than the little piggy barbecue?

The celebration begins at 12:00 with a kite-making party for the kids, followed by the Independence Day Parade at 2:00.

Funny Happenings Here

Then comes the kite-flying. There's good food, including world-class barbecue, arts and crafts, live music, and entertainment. Following a concert of beach music, the evening concludes with a spectacular fireworks display.

So next time someone asks you where you're going to celebrate the Fourth, tell 'em you're going where pigs fly!

Gold Rush Days Festival • McCormick

There's gold in them thar hills! Well, at least there was. According to legend, local planter William Dorn was out hunting one day in 1850 when his fox hounds discovered a vein of gold in the hills near present-day McCormick. Them's some pretty smart dogs, we say. Anyway, ol' Fool Billy, as he was known, wasn't so much a fool that he was going to let this opportunity pass. He staked his claim and began excavating, using slave labor. Within ten years, the Dorn Mine yielded up about a cool mil for Fool Billy, much of which he lost after the Civil War. In 1871, Cyrus McCormick the "father of farm mechanization" bought the mine for $20,000 and spent years trying to strike it rich. He never did. At least not with gold. Guess he did pretty well with that farm mechanization thing, though. The town that grew up around the mine is named for him.

Today, the town of McCormick celebrates its rich history with the annual Gold Rush Festival. There's a parade, arts and crafts, gold panning, tours of the Dorn Mine, and dancing.

Held annually in September.

GOVERNOR'S FROG JUMP • SPRINGFIELD

Feelin' froggy? Well, hop on over to Springfield, where you can participate in the annual Governor's Frog Jump. This storied festival has its roots in the Mark Twain story, "The Notorious Jumping Frog of Calaveras County," about a plain, old everyday frog that beats out the celebrated, educated frog in a jumping contest. The story was Twain's comment on the equality of people and that the civilized, educated one is not always the winner.

Rumor has it the Governor's Frog Jump got its start in South Carolina when then-governor Ronald Reagan challenged South Carolina's governor to a frog jumping contest. South Carolina's first frog jump was held in 1967 and, as a big hit, it soon became an annual event. It's been held in Springfield since 1969.

The main event of this froggy festival is, of course, the frog jumping contest, where champion frog jumpers and their champion frogs compete for the $750 first-place prize. They're also, no doubt, hoping to beat the all-time record jump of 21 feet 5.75 inches—a feat that would net them a hoppin' $5,000!

In addition to the official Frog Jump, there's the International Egg Striking Contest. Never heard of this particular competition? Us neither. It's really quite simple, though. The boiled egg that remains unbroken by the tapping of other eggs entered in the contest wins.

If those two contests don't appeal to ya, don't despair. There's a lot more to do. Try your hand at the Slingshot Contest, or the Horseshoe Contest. No, wait! How about that Cow Drop, where contestants predict just where said cow will make her "drop." Oh, such fun! There's also a really big parade, live entertainment, and dancing in the streets. It's toads, uh, loads of fun! Rrrrribbetttt!

Held annually in the spring.

GULLAH CELEBRATION • HILTON HEAD ISLAND

Gullah is a language. Gullah is a heritage. Gullah is a way of life. The Gullah culture originated on the Sea Islands of South Carolina and Georgia, when slaves were brought from South Africa to work the rice plantations. Many experts believe the name is derived from "Angola," where a large number of these slaves came from.

Because of the relative isolation of the Sea Islands and because the slaves here were allowed more self-sufficiency (they were left to man the plantations when the owners fled during the spring and summer malaria seasons), the Gullah language evolved and its traditions

A woman demonstrates indigo dyeing at the Gullah Celebration.
Courtesy of the HHI Gullah Celebration.

survived the centuries to enrich South Carolina's unique culture. Throughout Hilton Head and St. Helena islands, you'll find close-knit Gullah communities struggling to preserve their traditions in the face of wide-open global tourism.

The Gullah Celebration, recognized as a Southeast Top Twenty Event, showcases the many aspects of Gullah culture. Visitors journey through the culture, experiencing the art, food, music, and firsthand histories. The Arts, Crafts, and Food Expo gives an up-close and personal view of Gullah traditions, such as sweet grass basket sewing, indigo dyeing, and fishnet weaving. The Ol' Fashioned Gullah Barbecue offers traditional Gullah foods and cultural entertainment. There are storytellers and events such as the Gullah Praise, Stomp and Shout, African dancing, and Gospel music. The Gospel concerts highlight the history of the music, which has its roots in Gullah spirituals.

Held throughout the entire month of February.

IRIS FESTIVAL • SUMTER

South Carolina's oldest continuous festival, Sumter's Iris Festival is consistently ranked among the top festivals in the Southeast. The four-day festival includes concerts, an arts and crafts show, a flower show (of course!), a golf tournament, a food tasting, and the crowning of the Iris Festival King and Queen.

The festival takes place at Sumter's Crown Jewel, the Swan Lake-Iris Gardens, the history of which is rooted in the desire of a prominent Sumter businessman's lack of a green thumb. Back in 1927, Hamilton Bland wanted to landscape his yard with exotic Japanese Irises. Unfortunately, even with expert advice, Bland's irises refused to flourish. Dismayed and discouraged, he told his gardener to dig up the discontent irises and dump them in the thirty-acre cypress lake that happened to be on his property. Well, lo and behold, the next spring Bland was delighted to find that his discarded irises were all abloom on the edge of that lake. Bland later deeded his portion of the lake to the city to go with the 120-acre portion deeded previously by another prominent citizen. Today, the adjacent Iris Gardens encompass 150 acres bursting with a wide array of twenty-five varieties of colorful irises.

Swans? Oh, did we forget to mention them? Yes, Virginia, there are swans. They float placidly on the cypress-black waters of Swan Lake. The lake is home to all eight types of the world's swans, including exotics from Asia, Australia, England, and South America.

Held annually in May.

LOBSTER RACES • AIKEN

Naw, we ain't spoofin' you. OK, well, maybe we are...but, no lie, there really are lobster races in Aiken. The Lobster Races began, no doubt, as a spoof on Aiken's thoroughbred racing industry, which sponsors three weekends of racing in May. It's really just a way to get together and have some fun.

The Maine Lobster Thoroughbred Lobster Races take place at Lobster Downs, a unique saltwater track, where fans can cheer their favorite to victory. And, believe you me, this is a race the lobster really wants to win, for the winner goes free. All the rest are eaten!

In addition to the races, rides, family activities, live beach music, and gourmet food provided by local restaurants. And a good time is had by all—except those poor losing lobsters. But, dang it, they're good eatin'!

Held annually in May.

LOWCOUNTRY OYSTER FESTIVAL • CHARLESTON

Give me oysters and beer…for dinner everyday of the year…And I'll be fine…I'll feel fiiiine! Guess Jimmy Buffett says it best. Take a dozen slimy little bottom feeders, a little catsup, some horseradish—enough to clear your sinuses and make your eyes water—a squirt of lemon, and an ice cold beer, and you've just reached paradise.

Every year, the folks of Charleston celebrate the oyster by serving up bushels of them to thousands of people. If you don't like 'em raw, don't despair. You can get them fixed any way you want—fried, steamed, baked, broiled, and even stewed up in a delicious, creamy oyster stew.

If oysters aren't your cup of…stew, never fear. There's plenty of other food to be found. Live bands play rock, country, bluegrass, and beach music throughout the day. There's dancing in the streets, and an arts and crafts show. For the little kiddies, there's a best dressed oyster contest and lots of games and activities.

The big event of the Oyster Festival is the Oyster Shucking Contest, with amateur and professional divisions. You're probably thinking, oh, fun. But you'll be surprised just how exciting oyster shucking can be. And it has to be done just right, too. Shuckers receive penalties for damaging the oysters during shucking. Winners of the professional contest go to the

Funny Happenings Here

National Oyster Shucking Championship in Maryland and may advance to the World Oyster Shucking Championship in Ireland. Who knew?!

Held annually in January.

MOONSHINERS REUNION AND MOUNTAIN MUSIC FESTIVAL • CAMPOBELLO

Now here's a reunion you'll have a foot-stomping good time at. All right, we're going to come clean right off the bat. You won't find illegal liquor here. Them durn revenooers done put a stop to that. But, by golly, you ain't gonna miss it.

It was ol' Barney Barnwell that came up with the idea for this get together. See, he grew up listening to the tall tales of his moonshinin' relatives, and he wanted a way to keep that spirit alive. So he put together this two-day event at his Plum Hollow Farm, located in the "Dark Corners" of South Carolina. By featuring only local and regional bluegrass bands, ol' Barney keeps his festival true to its backwoods heritage.

You can come for the day if you want. But the most fun is when you camp. That way, you get to listen to musicians on stage and then at night when the show is over, you can sit by the campfire and pick a tune or listen whilst someone else picks a tune or two. Now that there's a good time!

Held annually the first weekend in October.

OKRA STRUT • IRMO

More than thirty years ago the little town of Irmo needed a new library, but there was no money. What can we do? I know!

We'll put on a festival! About okra! Folks will come from far and wide! They'll spend money! And, we'll have our library!

And so began the saga of Okraman. Yeah, it took several years for the giant okra to bring in enough money for a new library, but by that time, the Okra Strut had become one of South Carolina's biggest and best festivals. Today, the Okra Strut parade, with more than one hundred floats, is South Carolina's largest. The festival kicks off with a golf tournament on Friday and a popular street dance on Friday night. Saturday begins with the Dam Run out

Okra Man welcomes visitors to Okra Strut.
Courtesy of the Okra Strut Festival.

to the Lake Murray Dam, and after all that good exercise you won't feel guilty about stuffing yourself with fried okra and all the other goodies available.

Next comes the Orka Strut Parade and a day filled with all manner of entertainment: an okra-eating contest, puppet shows, arts and crafts, and a dunking booth. Best of all, festival goers can have there portraits made with Okra Man, a giant okra!

Held annually in September.

Funny Happenings Here

Pow Wow • Langley

Wow! It's a real pow wow. In traditional times, a pow wow was a gathering of one tribe of Native Americans, a social event, where they came together to hunt, plant, and celebrate. It was a time to renew family, clan, and tribal ties and was a way to strengthen and forge political and social alliances, celebrate victories, and to practice religious and spiritual ceremonies.

Today's pow wows have the same goals, but now they are a gathering of many tribes. They are an opportunity for Native Americans to celebrate their identity and express inter-tribal pride. By attending, you'll learn the history, culture, and traditions of the Indian people. And, you'll have lots of fun.

Sponsored by the Horse Creek American Indian Heritage Association, this pow wow features a weekend of fun. You'll see Native Americans in traditional dress drumming, singing, and dancing. There are also Indian crafts and Indian foods. It's a fun social event where you can meet old friends and make new ones.

Held in April and again in November.

Pumpkin Festival • Pumpkintown

Where else would you have a pumpkin festival? This little town, named for the giant pumpkins that grew here many years ago, celebrates the orange orb that inevitably brings to mind crisp days and mountainsides ablaze with fall colors. It's just a one-day celebration, but what a day!

There's, of course, the Pumpkin Parade, a greased pole climb, arts and crafts, and all kinds of food. Bring a chair or quilt and listen to the music and enjoy the performance of cloggers as their feet beat out a rhythm of the day.

Held annually in October.

ROCK AROUND THE CLOCK
• WINNSBORO

One, two, three o'clock, four o'clock rock…When the folks of Winnsboro say they're gonna rock around the clock, they mean it—literally. Winnsboro is home to the nation's oldest continuously running clock. Situated in the town square, this time honored miracle was built in 1833. It's ticked off nearly two hundred years of life in Winnsboro, where though the times have changed, you can still get a feel for days gone by.

Winnsboro's town clock is the nation's oldest continously running clock.
Courtesy of the Fairfield County Chamber of Commerce.

Winnsboro's Rock Around the Clock Festival is a rockin' little celebration of a town that takes pride in its laid back atmosphere, where the tourism theme is "Rocking Chair Memories." They invite you to jump off that speeding interstate and take a step back to a simpler time.

Funny Happenings Here

The folks of Winnsboro like their little rocking chair theme so well that to kick off the festivities, they stage a rocking chair parade. There is also an Old Fashioned Stump Meeting, live music, a wild and crazy street dance right there beneath the clock, food, a karaoke contest, car show, children's games, arts and crafts, tours of Winnsboro's South Carolina Railroad Museum, and a tennis tournament.

Held in October.

SOIREE • ANDERSON

Anderson's annual Soiree promotes partying in the streets. There's something for everyone. The kid's will be especially happy, with the Kid's Kingdom that's filled clowns and lots of activities, such as face painting and puppet shows. For the older kids, there's Teen World with music and stuff.

There are artists displaying and selling their work, all kinds of other stuff to see and buy, live music, and plenty of good food.

Held annually in April.

SOUTH CAROLINA FESTIVAL OF DISCOVERY • GREENWOOD

This little party is smokin'! First there's the smokin' of all those little piggies being cooked in the South Carolina State Barbecue Championship, featuring some of the best pig cookers in the country. There's also a traditional Black Kettle Hash cook off. Then there's all those smokin' musical instruments in the Blue Cruise, a series of five musical venues featuring some of the country's cookin'est musicians.

Learn all about South Carolina here, from her food to her music to her artistry and to her fun. In addition to the 'round-the-clock food and music, there are arts and crafts shows, marionette shows, a carnival for the kid in us all, a hot dog eating contest, and tours of the Greenwood Railroad Museum and the Greenwood

The Black Kettle Hash Cook-Off is one of the activities at the South Carolina Festival of Discovery.
Courtesy of the Uptown Greenwood Development Corporation.

Museum. No matter how much you know, you'll make discoveries here. Perhaps you'll discover what you love about the Palmetto State.

Held annually in July.

SPITTOONO FESTIVAL • CLEMSON

The Spittoono Festival got its start in 1981 when a group of good ol' boys were sitting around at the Esso, Clemson's gas station-turned-bar, when someone brought up Charleston's upscale Spoleto Festival. Someone else allowed how he'd much prefer to be kicked by a mule than to sit around watching guys in tights leap around a stage to Italian music.

What was needed, they decided, was a real man's festival, where real men could do real-man things like chug beer and crush the cans on their foreheads and see who could spit tobacco the farthest. Now that would be a festival. They'd have cheap beer and real musicians playing real-man instruments, such as guitars, banjos, and drums. No cellos and no tights allowed. And so the Spittoono was born.

Conceived of and sponsored by the Redneck Performing Arts Association, the Spittoono has emerged as the premier redneck event. Cheap beer. Good music. Spittin'. Chuggin'. It's redneck heaven. Bet some o' them Spoleto folks sneak in too, get a break from all that tights-wearin'.

Best thing about the Spittoono is admission is free and all proceeds from beer and food sales go to local charities, to help "kids and critters." So, start workin' out those spittin' muscles and make plans to attend.

Held annually in August.

South Carolina is the birthplace of two famous Jacksons. Andrew Jackson, the seventh U.S. president, was born in Waxhaws on March 15, 1767. The Reverend Jesse Jackson, a civil rights activist, was born in Greenville on October 8, 1941.

SPOLETO FESTIVAL USA • CHARLESTON

Charleston's Spoleto Festival is a world famous event. It began in 1977 as an American counterpart to the storied Festival of Two Worlds, which began in Spoleto, Italy in 1958. The organizers of that festival chose Charleston for the new festival because of its old-world charm, and its wealth of theaters, churches, and performance venues.

The Spoleto Festival has maintained the Festival of Two World's dedication to young artists and its commitment to the performing arts. For seventeen days every year, the Spoleto Festival fills Charleston's historic theaters, churches, and outdoor venues with performances by well-known artists, as well as performances by up and coming new performers. The more than 120 presentations run the gamut of the performing arts. You can enjoy opera, theater, music theater, visual arts, and chamber, symphonic, choral, and jazz music. Firmly established as one of the world's top art festivals, it is the largest of its kind in the country.

Held annually in May.

SPRING COOTER FEST • ALLENDALE

"Cooter" is the term given to a class of turtles composed of eight species that live in various aquatic habitats. Found mostly in the Central and Southeastern states, they prefer quiet canal waters, lakes, and ponds. Most of Allendale's cooters are found in ditches and ponds.

The Carolina Cooter Race takes place during the Spring Cooter Fest, and if you can't catch your own cooter, you can rent one for the race. The cooters are raced in division heats until there's a winner and at the end of the day, the winners of the divisions race for the grand title of "The Fastest Cooter." A one thousand dollar prize comes with the title. So get out there and find you a cooter! Just remember, trying to increase speed by placing any foreign substance, such as oil, on your cooter will result in immediate disqualification.

Funny Happenings Here

Oh! But the race is just one small part of the Spring Cooter Fest! There's a beauty pageant. There are carnival rides. There's a parade. There's food. There's lots and lots of music. There's dancing in the streets. And it all ends with a fireworks extravaganza. Whew! It's a fun-packed weekend.

Held the first week in April.

Did you know you could travel the globe without ever leaving South Carolina? You can visit Denmark, La France, New Holland, Norway, Scotia, Switzerland, Bath, Lancaster, Windsor, York, Waterloo, Warsaw Island, Florence, Bordeaux, and Parris Island.

You'll find lots of towns to rest in during your travels. First off, you'll be welcomed in Welcome. And, then there's Traveler's Rest, Fountain Inn, Lodge, Bath, and Hickory Tavern. There's also plenty of running water: Boiling Springs, Cool Spring, Springdale, Allsbrook, Brooksville, Forestbrook, and Seabrook.

You can go in any direction: Due West, Eastover, South Congaree, and North. Huh. North, South Carolina, could get confusing.

SUGARFOOT CLASSIC • HONEA PATH

Who knew? Who knew there were that many horseshoe pitchers out there? Who knew there was a National Horseshoe Pitchers Association? Who knew there was even a horseshoe pitchers hall of fame?

Well, the good folks of Honea Path knew. For several years now, the town has been hosting the Sugarfoot Classic Horseshoe Pitching Tournament, an event that draws champion horseshoe pitchers from all over the Southeast. Well, folks, all we can say is it's gotta be more fun than watchin' golf.

Of course, if horsepitching's not your cuppa, you can attend the Sugarfoot Festival that runs concurrent with the tournament. The streets of Honea Path are turned into an old country fair with music, food, games, hayrides, fireworks, and an annual honey soppin.' Now that's a sweet time.

Held annually in October.

WORLD GRITS FESTIVAL • ST. GEORGE

Know how mom used to tell you to quit playing with your food? Well, pack up mom and bring her to the St. George, where you can not only play in your food, you can jump in and roll around in it! You might even win some money doing it.

It's all part of the World Grits Festival, a three-day event that has gained national attention for the town of St. George, the self-proclaimed Grits Capital of the World. The whole thing started back in 1985, when a couple of grits vendors mentioned to the manager of the local Piggly Wiggly that they sure did deliver a lot of grits to his store. A little checking and the manager discovered that indeed, the little town of two thousand did eat more grits per capita than any other town in the world.

The festival kicks off with a parade and there's music, dancing in the streets, a clothesline art show, arts and crafts, a carnival, lots of food (including of course grits), on-site grits grinding, and performances by square dancers, cloggers, and line dancers. You can also try your hand at a few of the contests, such as the Corn Tossing Contest, the Corn Shelling Contest (Y'all did know that grits are made from corn, right?), and the Grits Eating Contest.

Now all that's fun, but the main event at the World's Grits Festival is, without a doubt, the Roll in the Quaker Grits Contest, where contestants jump into a big ol' vat of cooked grits and roll around for ten seconds. The contestant emerging with the most grits sticking to him wins.

The World Grits Festival was recently named a Top Twenty Event in the Southeast. Every year, more than forty-five thousand folks come join in the fun. What could be better? You can have your grits and roll in 'em, too!

Held annually in April.

Strange But True Culture

Artists, world-class writers, and music men—it's culture with a twist in Strange But True South Carolina.

Artists

Folk Artists. Self-taught Artists. Outsiders. Whatever you call them, it's been said that there's just one rule in folk art: The artist must be as interesting as his art. That's not a problem here!

RICHARD BURNSIDE • PENDLETON

Richard has visions. They come to him late at night and refuse to leave until he puts them to canvas. OK, well, maybe not to canvas. Sometimes he paints on cardboard; sometimes on scraps of metal. He's even been known to paint on gourds. Although his favorite canvas is plywood, Burnside will paint on whatever's handy when the visions come.

Born in Baltimore in 1944, he moved with his family to South Carolina when he was five years old. When he was older, he worked for several years at the S&H Greenstamps store in Greenville. Then joined the army in 1974, where he says he was disappointed that he wasn't sent overseas. After his discharge in 1978, he spent time as a chef in Charlotte, North Carolina, and it was here that the visions began. Feeling compelled by God, he began painting the scenes that kept him awake at night. In 1983, he returned to South Carolina.

Burnside now lives in Pendleton, where he spends his time creating the unique images from his visions of "ancient times." His works are primal, favoring images of ancient kings, queens, jungle cats, bugs, and wolves. Many of his paintings are adorned personal symbols only he knows the meaning of. Many of these symbols take

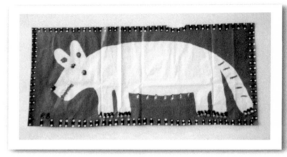

Robert Burnside created *White Wolf* in 1990.
Courtesy of Robert Cargo Folk Art Gallery in Paoli, PA.

the form of snakes and spiders, while others are from an ancient language he calls the "Roman Alphabet."

Although most of his work reflects the African-American culture, some animals and figures resemble those found in Navajo sand paintings. A recurring figure in Burnside's work is that of a round, flat face, often surrounded by long white hair. It is seen in many different colors, against many backgrounds, and is usually surrounded by Burnside's Roman Alphabet. The face, he says, is his most prominent recurring vision.

"Got to obey God," Burnside says of his reason for putting paint to…whatever. "This art, it never existed until it came out of me." Today, Burnside's work is well-known and much-touted in the art world. His pieces can be found hanging in museums and in private and public collections around the country.

L.C. CARSON • ORANGEBURG

Like many folk artists, L.C. Carson came to the art world late in life. He had spent the majority of his adult life as a successful builder and was civic leader in his hometown of Orangeburg. After retiring in the early 1970s, Carson soon realized he needed something to do with his time. A trip to Alabama provided the inspiration for a new chapter in his life. During that trip, he toured Ave Maria Grotto, a four-acre park containing 125 miniature reproductions of famous world buildings, made completely of discarded materials and constructed in exquisite detail by Benedictine monk Brother Joseph Zoettl in the 1930s.

Carson was captivated. Upon his return, he began construction of his Concrete City. Using the skills he had gained in the construction business and a vast array of materials, he constructed thirty-three models of buildings from around the world in his backyard. Included were the Parthenon, Notre Dame Cathedral, the Sphinx, and the Colosseum. In addition to his Concrete City, he also created wood carvings of figures from folklore, mythology, and popular culture. Among them you'll find the Lizard Man of Lee County, a Mayan God, a portrait of Bill Clinton, and a whimsical self portrait.

Carson died in 1998, but his work lives on. The entire city and his collection of carvings, save one, have been moved to the South Carolina State Museum.

Strange But True Culture

KIM CLAYTON • MYRTLE BEACH

Kim Clayton's not your usual idea of a folk artist. She's young. She's blonde. She's pretty. But folk artist she is, using her self-taught skills to create artwork that challenges one to look inward and find the beauty in all things. Much of her subject matter speaks to empowerment, primarily of women, but it also speaks of her passion for giving of herself. She's active in causes for the physically impaired, for children, and the homeless.

Like many folk artists, she a consummate recycler, scouring junkyards for castoffs, such as refrigerator doors and old windows, to transform into beautiful and insightful works of art. Her strong linework, inspiring messages, and use of brilliant colors have gained her a large following throughout the east coast and in Chicago, New York, and New Orleans.

Clayton lives in Myrtle Beach, where she has a studio and a gallery. The Blackwater Gallery is located in nearby Conway. Take a visit and you can't miss it. The renovated Main Street brick building is covered with Clayton's vivid, whimsical artwork.

SILAS DEKIND • PLANTERSVILLE

Hard times affect people differently. For some the hard times become a hammer that beats them down. Others take that hammer and beat the hard times into art that touches the world. Silas DeKind was one who didn't let the hard times get him down. When the career truck driver sustained a disabling spinal injury, he just decided it was time to change direction.

As a child Silas had been interested in art, and even went so far as to engage in competitions with his mother to see who could draw the best. Then he grew up and had grown up responsibilities. Had to make a living. Couldn't be playing around with crayons. But, suddenly, here he was with all this time on his hands and he realized his new direction would take him to a place he'd been before.

DeKind began making artwork that was way beyond the drawings he made as a child. Gathering up plywood, pine, twigs, frayed rope, paint, and all manner of found materials, he began creating three-dimensional works of art. He grew up in the South, and it's the images of that region that inspire much of his art. In large detailed wood carvings, embellished with his found objects, he often depicts scenes of baptism and other spiritual themes. "Baptisms are big things," he's said. "They're giving it up for God. And I like that." Other favorite themes include Lowcountry landscapes, scenes of plantation life, and carvings of Egyptians princesses and Pharaohs.

Dekind's work appears in museums around South Carolina and in Washington, D.C.

SAM DOYLE • ST. HELENA ISLAND

Sam Doyle's artwork is a chronicle of life on St. Helena Island. Born there in 1906, he lived his entire life in the small community of Frogmore. His talent for art was noticed early on, and a childhood teacher offered him the opportunity to go to New York to study art. Doyle turned down the offer, partly because of the impoverishment of his family and partly because he didn't want to leave his home.

During the years of his childhood and youth, St. Helena Island was an isolated community, populated entirely by blacks, most descendants of freed slaves. It wasn't until 1927 that a bridge finally connected the island to Beaufort. Doyle dropped out of school in the ninth grade to work as a clerk in a neighborhood store. Later, he found work in Beaufort as a porter, where he worked between 1930 and 1950, and as a laundry worker on Parris Island Marine Corps, where he worked for sixteen years.

In 1968, Doyle renewed his interest in art. He began painting, using house paint and large wooden panels or pieces of castoff roofing tin, when available, and anything he could get his hands on. He's painted on everything from corrugated board to window shades.

The subject of Doyle's work was St. Helena life. He filled his yard with paintings of her citizens, her places, her history. He dedicated the last fifteen years of his life to preserving and commemorating the rich heritage of this Gullah community. One of his favorite subjects was Dr. Buzzard, or Dr. Buz, as he was known, a voodoo doctor who was St. Helena's wealthiest citizen. He also painted a series of St. Helena "firsts," the first football game played on St. Helena, the island's first doctor, the first midwife, etc. Doyle also painted scenes of every day life on St. Helena as well as religious works and paintings of famous folks, such as Elvis Presley and Ray Charles.

He filled his back yard with his powerful paintings, placing them side by side against the fencing, against a building, and displayed on the ground. Interspersed with the paintings and edging the perimeter of his outdoor gallery, Doyle had placed sculptures of snakes, reptiles, birds, and other animals. Made from tree limbs, driftwood, and scraps of lumber, they were simple affairs adorned with feathers and other found materials. These sculptures, many believe, were made to protect the highly superstitious Doyle from evil spirits.

Since his death in 1985, Doyle's work has received much attention from the folk art world, with his paintings now being displayed in museums across the Southeast.

MADISON LATIMER • PIEDMONT AREA

Madison Latimer is a chicken lady. No, I'm not saying she's a coward. Far from it. Latimer is, indeed, a brave woman, a woman who endured a tragic loss, but found a way to heal her own pain and a way to help others heal and remember to celebrate life. And she does it with chickens.

In 1995, Latimer lost three dear family members to a traffic accident. In healing the pain of that loss, she says she began to understand and feel the connection of the "energy that provides life." She became aware that all things are connected to an "eternal force" from which all things come. She understood this, but was at a loss as to how to express it to others.

Then one morning, while looking out the window of her Piedmont-area farmhouse, she happened to see a chicken "just being happy," and she was hit smack in the face with an epiphany. Epiphanies have been known to do that, you know. Especially those chicken epiphanies. Anyhoo, by seeing this chicken kicking up its little heels and having a chickie good time, Latimer saw a way to express to others her belief in the connection and continuation of the life force in us all. She began to paint chickens. No, silly. She paints them on a canvas.

But these aren't just plain old Rhode Island Reds. Heaven forbid! No, Latimer's chickens are vividly colored and prodigiously plumed. Some wear expressions of joy, some seem startled, most seem happy. They all seem to celebrate life. And, that's Latimer's goal with her art: To help people celebrate life.

Madison Latimer paints to help people enjoy life.
Courtesy of Madison Latimer.

GENE MERRITT • ROCK HILL

Gene Merritt's life has been rock hard. Born into a violent and alcoholic family, he suffered a severe bout of pneumonia that left him brain damaged at an early age. His mother committed suicide when Merritt was twelve and he moved with his father from Columbia to Fort Hill. During the day, he worked odd jobs—shoe shiner, packer in a grocery store, ticket taker at a theater, etc.—and at night he and his father fought and drank.

In 1972, Merritt's father died and he was left under the supervision of social services, who placed him with a family who was charged with caring for him. The family, instead, left him on his own in a trailer out behind their house, where he lived for fifteen years.

Merritt began drawing in 1992, mostly ballpoint pen sketches of popular culture. An avid television watcher, he drew portraits of characters he saw on TV, rock stars, political icons, and movie stars. His portraits were unusual, drawn disjointed, with faces segmented by lines as in a jigsaw puzzle. He inscribes the name of the subject (often misspelled), dates it—sometimes dated in the future—and signs it "Gene's Art's Inc."

Watkins Grille in Rock Hill served as his studio, and he often traded his drawings for coffee or a meal in those early days. It wasn't long, however, before his drawings were noticed by folk art collectors and soon his work was in demand and being displayed in local museums and collections.

Today, Merritt's life isn't so hard. He lives in a house provided for him and spends his days drawing. His work has gained international fame with the sale of fifty-nine drawings to the Switzerland's Collection de l'Art Brut, one of the world's most prestigious folk art museums.

PHILIP SIMMONS • CHARLESTON

Philip Simmons was eight years old the first time he stepped into a blacksmith shop, and for the first moment he was captivated. He loved all the action, sparks flying, the pounding of hammers, horses neighing. He begged for a job—anything, shoe shining, sweeping up, whatever. Come back when you're thirteen, he was told. The day after he turned thirteen, he returned to that same shop. And he stayed for the next sixty years.

Simmons started out shoeing horses. But, then along came the automobile, and folks didn't have horses anymore. So he started making trailers and car hitches. But then, factories started turning those out cheaper than he could make them. Now what? Serendipity. Simmons had moved his shop out to the waterfront, where the heavy salt air was hard on the ornamental iron. One day a lady asked if he could repair her gate. And, so, a new profession was born. He began making repairs to important ornamental iron pieces around Charleston, including the historic Sword Gate and the gate at St. Michael's cemetery. Seeing these designs sparked an inspiration to create designs of his own.

Taking hammer to hot metal, he began fashioning more than functional pieces, he began making art. Within the heavy confines of a metal gate he captured the delicacy of nature's designs, egrets, fish, snakes, stars, moons, leaves, and the lacy curves of water. His artistry caught notice and soon his work was being hung as gates, fences, balconies, and window grills throughout Charleston.

Now well into his nineties, Simmons is a state treasure, well-loved and well-recognized for his artistry. In 1982, the National Endowment for the Arts awarded him the National Heritage Fellowship, the highest honor that can be bestowed upon a traditional artist. He also was awarded a Lifetime Achievement Award by South Carolina, was inducted into the South Carolina Hall of Fame, received the Order of the Palmetto (South Carolina's highest award) and the Elizabeth O'Neill Verner Governor's Award for Lifetime Achievement in the Arts. His work is displayed in the National Museum of American History; the Smithsonian Institute; the Museum of International Folk Art in Santa Fe, New Mexico; the South Carolina State Museum; the Richland County Library in Columbia; and the Atlanta History Center in Atlanta, Georgia.

DALTON STEVENS • BISHOPVILLE

When someone tells Dalton Stevens to "button it," he's got the hardware to do it. Many years ago, Stevens, a chronic insomniac, needed something to occupy his time while not being able to sleep. Guess he had a wealth of buttons lying around and for some reason, he decided to start sewing them onto a suit. Hmm. Going without sleep sure will make you punchy, we guess.

Anyway, two years, ten months, and countless sleepless nights later, Stevens had a suit with 16,333 buttons sewn onto it. And still he couldn't sleep. He started gluing buttons to all sorts of things. He glued buttons to guitars and pianos. He glued 600,000 of them on to a hearse and 149,000 to a Chevrolet Chevette. Oh, and then there's the outhouse and the two caskets—one of which Stevens says will be his final resting place, where we're assuming he'll finally get some sleep!

Stevens has won national fame for his insomnia cure, appearing numerous time on the *Tonight Show with Johnny Carson*, *The David Letterman Show*, and *Nashville Now with Ralph Emery*. Although he's no longer making his button creations, he has opened a small museum between Bishopville and Camden to show them off. Admission is free, though donations are accepted.

Strange But True Culture

WILLIAM THOMAS THOMPSON • GREENVILLE

It's no wonder that during a church service in Hawaii back in 1989 Harry Thompson experienced a fiery vision of the Apocalypse. It was, it seems, the end of the world as Thompson knew it. Not only had the former-millionaire just lost his fortune but he also had been stricken by a mysterious illness that had paralyzed him from the knees down and weakened the use of his hands and arms.

Immediately after the vision, Thompson, who'd never created art of any kind, began painting. Once returning to his Greenville home he began filling the place with frighteningly vivid paintings of the end

William Thomas Thompson calls his style of painting "Art in the Midst of Rage."
Courtesy of William Thomas Thompson, Thompson-art.com

of the world. He's painted more than 600 pieces, most filled with religious images. In addition, he's painted a 150-foot mural of the book of Revelations that hangs in the foyer of the EXPLO building in Lausanne, Switzerland, and a 300-foot version that has been exhibited in museums across the U.S.

Painting on an upper-floor ballroom of his home, the Gassaway Mansion, Thompson has found ways to accommodate the physical limitations caused by his Guillain-Barre disease. With his large canvases spread in front of him on the floor, he mixes his acrylics on the canvas and paints quickly. The wavy, unsteady lines with bountiful lettering are a trademark and are a result of his physical impairment.

Thompson says he creates from rage—not rage of anger, but rage of rapture, fury, and belief. It's the rage he says that pushes the brush and Thompson and the paint along with it. "Art in the Midst of Rage" he calls its.

Visual art, says Thompson, is one of the greatest communicators. It is a gift from God, through which he hopes to spread the word of right.

INEZ NATHANIEL WALKER • SUMTER

Well, talk about your hard times. Inez Nathaniel Walker was born into poverty in Sumter in 1911. Orphaned early in life, she married at sixteen and had four kids right away. She moved to Philadelphia to get away from the rigors of farm work—though we can't imagine that working in a pickle factory was a whole lot better. The pickle factory closed and things only got worse for our Inez. She went to migrant farm work, traveling through New York, living variously in Clyde, Geneva, and Savannah. Guess the capper came when she was sentenced to prison in the early 1970s for killing a man who had abused her. You know, life happens.

Anyway, with three hots and a cot, Inez was finally free to let her creative side out. She began sketching stylized drawings, mostly of women whose heads were larger than their bodies.

They invariably had intricate hairdos and large eyes. Often they were dressed in patterned clothing.

One day, Walker left a number of the drawings in the prison mess hall, where they were discovered by the prison's remedial English teacher, who showed them to the art teacher, who supplied Walker with art supplies and showed her work to an art dealer. Walker became quite prolific, filling sketch book after sketch book, and by her release in 1972, she had enough for a show. And, the rest, as they say, is history.

Walker died in 1990, but her work lives on. She's included in the *Rosenak Encyclopedia* and in *Black Folk Art in America 1930-1980*. Her work is displayed in such faraway and prestigious places as the Collection de l'Art Brut in Lausanne, Switzerland, and the L'Arcanie, Neuilly-sur-Marne in France. Whew! Can't get that far? You can also see Walker's work at the Museum of American Folk Art in New York; the Museum of International Folk Art in Santa Fe, New Mexico; and the Smithsonian Institute in Washington, D.C.

ZENOBIA WASHINGTON • GEORGETOWN

Zenobia Washington is another self-taught artist doing her part to preserve the Gullah tradition. After the death of her brother left her in a deep depression, Washington turned to doll-making as art therapy. Like Vermelle Rodriguez, Washington makes dolls of strong women. "Women of Inspiration," she calls them.

Rather than women she knows, Washington's dolls are representative of women of African-American and Gullah heritage. Among the many dolls, you'll find the Quilter doll, who keeps the history; the Going-to-Market doll that pays homage to all women; and the Black Widow, a regal but forbidding doll that symbolizes the widows of lynching victims.

An important characteristic of all of Washington's dolls is the fact that they are all faceless. This, she says, is because the African-American women were historically faceless. Abused, ignored, and used, they nevertheless were, and are, beautiful and talented.

Music from the Heart

In 1762, Charlestown became the home of the St. Cecelia Society, America's first musical society. And things never stopped rockin'. South Carolina is the birthplace, in fact, of two of Rock's pioneers, men who heard the beat and started the world dancing to it.

JAMES BROWN • BARNWELL

Who could ever forget James Brown, the Godfather of Soul? He was a sight, with his trademark page boy and an awful leisure suit. But, man, could he rock. And sing. In that voice you could hear his hard times.

Born in Barnwell, he picked cotton in the nearby fields and shined shoes downtown to help support his family. As he grew, he began committing petty crimes and at age sixteen, found himself doing time in a juvenile detention center for armed robbery. It changed his life, for here he met lifetime friend

Bobby Byrd, who helped him get an early release and introduced him to music.

During the mid and early 1950s, Brown performed in gospel groups then graduated into rhythm and blues. Into the 1960s, he began innovating with the music and vocals. Adding in live performances that incorporated dance with spins, drops, and splits, he jacked up the intensity of R&B and morphed it into a whole new sound called Funk. In 1965, he scored his first Number One hit with "Papa's Got a Brand New Bag," followed immediately by "I Got You (I Feel Good)." He continued to score with hits every decade through 1980.

In 2006, he completed his "Seven Decades of Funk World Tour," which was his last. He remained popular to the end, with his last concert attracting a record crowd of eighty thousand people.

On Christmas Day 2006, Brown died from congestive heart failure resulting from complications of pneumonia. According to his friend, Charles Bobit, who was present at Brown's death, the legend said, "I'm going away tonight," and then took three long breaths and died.

CHUBBY CHECKER • SPRING GULLEY

OK, admit it, if we'd put Ernest Evans as the headline, you woulda said "Who?" Evans was born in little Spring Gulley, but raised in South Philadelphia. He got his start in show business early, forming a street corner harmony group at the age of eleven. By the time he'd entered high school, he could play a little piano and could do vocal impressions. By this time, he'd earned the nickname "Chubby," for obvious reasons. He decided to take the stage name "Chubby Checkers" as a take on then-popular singer Fats Domino.

Chubby enjoyed performing and entertained classmates and coworkers at the Fresh Farm Poultry store where he worked. His boss was so impressed that he arranged for Chubby to do a yuletide recording of his impression of different singers singing "Jingle Bells," for Dick Clark (yes, THE Dick Clark), who sent it out as a Christmas greeting to all his friends. This led to Chubby's 1960 blockbuster hit recording "The Twist."

Come on, baby. Let's do the twist! Not only did Chubby have a hit on his hands, but he had also introduced a whole new concept in dancing—a concept he called "dancing apart to the beat." The Twist, the first dance where partners didn't touch became a wild craze and spawned all kinds of new dances—Remember? The Pony? The Jerk? The Monkey? Oh! Oh! Remember the Bugaloo? Oh, hush. You're too young to remember.

Anyway, "The Twist" was a Number One hit in 1960, then returned to hit Number One again in 1962, the only record to ever hit Number One twice. Chubby kept turning out similar hits, and in later life he lamented that the phenomenal success of "The Twist" had ruined his life. He had wanted a career as a nightclub singer, but no one wanted to hear other types of music from him or believed that he truly had talent.

Success is relative, we guess. For though, he may have seen "The Twist" as his downfall, the fact remains he is the only artist to ever have five albums in the Top Twelve at once and the only artist to have a song become Number One twice. And, best of all, he changed the way the world danced. How much more successful can you be?

Writers

South Carolina lays claim to three of the country's most popular writers. They're a varied trio. You got your hard-boiled type. There's the man of history. And there's the tortured soul whose words evoke the very heart of the Lowcountry.

PAT CONROY • BEAUFORT

"To describe our growing up in the lowcountry of South Carolina, I would have to take you to the marsh on a spring day, flush the blue heron from its silent occupation, scatter marsh hens as we sink to our knees in mud, open you an oyster with a pocketknife and feed it to you from the shell and say, 'There. That taste. That's the taste of my childhood.' I would say, 'Breathe deeply,' and you would breathe and remember that smell for the rest of your life, the bold, fecund aroma of the tidal marsh, exquisite and sensual, the smell of the South in heat, a smell like new milk, semen, and spilled wine, all perfumed with seawater. My soul grazes like a lamb on the beauty of indrawn tides."

Pat Conroy didn't grow up in South Carolina, but you'd never know it from reading his novels. Even if you've never set foot inside the borders, as you read his words, you can feel the sun bronzing your upturned face and sense the tidal marshes tugging at your heart.

Conroy credits his love of language to his mother, a Southern woman, who despite being controlling and manipulative, inspired in her son a love of nature. His father, a Marine fighter pilot, was a violent man who often abused his children. "In our family, I love you was said with fists," Conroy has said. The lasting effect of his difficult childhood is a recurring theme of his books.

As a military brat, Conroy lived on military bases throughout the South. He changed schools eleven times in twelve years, finally attending the Citadel, where he was captain and most valuable player of the Varsity basketball team. While there, he wrote and published his first book, *The Boo*, a tribute to a favorite teacher.

After graduation, he decided to claim Beaufort as home, teaching English for a time then accepting a teaching position at a one-room schoolhouse on Daufuskie Island, where he taught underprivileged children. He was fired after a year for such offenses as refusing to allow corporal punishment and a lack of respect for administration. His experiences here became the subject of his second book, *The Water is Wide*, which was published in 1972. As with all his books, he wrote with brutal honesty, exposing the prevailing racism and the appalling conditions of the school. The book won him a humanitarian award from the National Education Association. It was made into a movie entitled *Conrack*, the nickname given to him by his students.

In 1976, Conroy's novel *The Great Santini* was published. An autobiographical novel that gave an honest portrayal of the brutality of his father, the book caused him much pain. He has said he underestimated the reactions of his family. The fallout caused not only his own divorce, but also the divorce of his parents. The animosity from his family lasted for years. In the movie inspired by the book, Robert Duvall gave a powerful performance that won him an Oscar nomination.

In his next novel, *The Lords of Discipline*, Conroy turned his candor on his alma mater, exposing the bigotry, sexism, and harsh military discipline of the school. His account ruffled some military feathers, and for a while, he was disowned by the school. This book, too, was made into movie, as was his next book.

If when you hear *The Prince of Tides*, you think only of the movie starring Barbra Streisand and Nick Nolte, then you are sadly deprived. The movie covers only a minute portion of this epic story, Conroy's masterpiece, and my most favorite book ever. To cover the entire story of the profoundly dysfunctional Wingo family, a movie would have to be four hours long. And, still, it would not be enough. A movie would deny you the ineffable pleasure of curling up in a favorite place and allowing Conroy to peel away the layers of his tale one by one, while his lyrical prose sings to you of shrimpers and turtles and tigers, and a secret so dark it can never be remembered. Never should you deny yourself such pleasure.

After *The Prince of Tides*, came *Beach Music*, a tale of trauma that reaches back to the Vietnam War and the Holocaust. Published in 1995, it was a book that, combined with the suicide of his brother, drove Conroy to the brink of a breakdown.

In his most recent book, *My Losing Season*, Conroy returns to his days as the captain of the Citadel's basketball team. A true account of his last season there, it's a story about losing and the lessons it teaches and about finding oneself in the midst of defeat.

Today, if he hasn't completely exorcised the demons of his childhood, Conroy says he has at least made peace. He was able to heal the rifts with both his parents before their deaths and even his alma mater has forgiven him. The college recently bestowed an honorary degree upon him.

Conroy was first introduced to Fripp Island as a teenager, when his mother chose it as a family summer getaway. Its beach, he says, was "an abundant, profligate text that never tired of serving up mysteries" to explore. He's still exploring mysteries there, in a home facing a salt water lagoon that daily serves up a panoply of natural beauty.

"Because I came to Beaufort County as a boy, my novels all smell of seawater. I watch things closely here, and try to get the details right. I write about the great salt marshes and pretend I am the marsh. I do the same with the ocean, the horseshoe crab, the flock of brown pelicans, and the beach-strewn kelp, the half-eaten stingray. I try to inhabit the soul of thing before I write about them, the way my mother taught me."

JOHN JAKES • HILTON HEAD

By the time he came to South Carolina in 1989 as a research fellow at the University of South Carolina, John Jakes was already known as "the godfather of the historical novel" and

"America's history teacher." His 1970s eight-volume series, *The Kent Family Chronicles*, which depicted American history through the lives of a fictional family, was a publishing phenomenon in the decade of the American Bicentennial. With this series, Jakes became the first author to have three books on the New York Times bestseller list in a single year. All eight volumes were bestsellers. Next came the Civil War trilogy, all of which were bestsellers and all of which were made into television miniseries.

Although he's most well-known for his historical fiction, Jakes has written in a number of genres. He started out writing short stories for pulp magazine, having sold his first for $25 at age eighteen, an event that changed the course of his life. Up until that time, he had planned to become an actor. He's written two hundred short stories and more than sixty books in genres as varied as mystery, science fiction, and western.

Jakes' historical book, *Charleston*, was published in 2002. An epic novel, the story introduces the fictional Bell family and follows their tale from the 1720s through the Civil War. His reason for choosing Charleston as the base for his story, says Jakes, lies in its importance to American history. The city—and the South—played a pivotal role in the first two hundred years of our country. Because at the time America was an agricultural nation, the leading agricultural states, such as South Carolina and Virginia, dominated national politics until the rise of the industrial shifted power to the North.

Although he chose writing over acting, he did not abandon his dreams of the stage. Jakes has remained actively involved in theater. He has acted and directed, as well as written original plays and musical. He has been especially active in the theater of Hilton Head, where he now resides. He's acted in many plays there and in 2003 he wrote new text and scenes for the ballet *La Boutique Fantasque*, which premiered at the Hilton Head Dance Theater at Christmas.

Jakes says he finds his role as America's history teacher a gratifying one. He takes satisfaction in letters and comments he receives from his fans, crediting him with inspiring an interest in history. The most gratifying comments, he says, are ones from fans who were inspired to become history teachers because of his books.

MICKEY SPILLANE • MURRELLS INLET

His name was Frank Morrison Spillane aka Mickey Spillane. His alter ego, Mike Hammer, a tough-guy gumshoe with a penchant for violence and long-pinned dames. Together, these two brunos helped to define the hard-boiled detective genre.

Born in Brooklyn, New York in 1918, Spillane created Hammer in his own physical image—a six-foot-four bear of a man. He, in fact, portrayed his creation in at least one of the movies made from his books. One suspects, hopes even, that elements of Hammer's psyche were a complete fabrication.

Introduced in Spillane's 1947 *I, the Jury*, Hammer out-toughs the other hard-boiled detectives of the time, a pretty hard group that included Sam Spade and Philip Marlowe. He was brutally violent, chauvinistic to the point of misogyny, and filled with a rage, guided only by blind devotion to "justice." Trusting neither coppers nor shysters, he preferred to settle matters with his own rough justice, pulling his roscoe and pumping lead into the bad guys at a drop of his lid.

Considering himself a "writer" not an author, Spillane poo-pooed the critics who panned his work. "But it's good garbage," was his reply, laughing, no doubt, all the way to the bank. He reveled in his status as America's most popular writer, a fact confirmed by a 1967 audit showing seven of the top ten best-selling books of the twentieth century as his.

Although tame by today's standards, Spillane's books contained considerably more violence and sexual episodes than his contemporaries' tomes. A product of his time, Hammer and his extreme patriotism struck a cord with a generation anxious over communism and facing a frightening new world. There were thirteen Mike Hammer books, five of which were made into movies, a comic strip, and several radio and television series based on the character. His popularity lasted even into the nineties, with Hammer being revived (both literally, from two gunshots to the gut, and figuratively, from an almost ten-year hiatus) in the 1996 *The Black Alley*.

Spillane began his career in 1935, writing for comic books such as *Captain Marvel*, *Superman*, *Batman*, and *Captain America*. In the 1960s, he jumped on the James Bond bandwagon with his *Tiger Mann*, a series based on a character who works for an espionage organization funded by a right-wing billionaire.

A long-time resident, Spillane came to Murrells Inlet in 1954 after falling in love with the long stretches of then-deserted beaches he glimpsed from an airplane. He lived there for more than thirty years, watching as South Carolina's tobacco and corn fields were plowed under to make way for tourist attractions, condos, and motels and living through 1989's Hurricane Hugo, which demolished his home. He died on Murrells Inlet on July 17, 2006.